IN GOD'S RECONCILING GRACE

Prayer and reflection texts
for Christian reconciliation and unity

Bernard de Margerie
Author and Editor

Preface by Bishop Donald Bolen

Library and Archives Canada Cataloguing in Publication

De Margerie, Bernard, 1934-, author, editor
    In God's reconciling grace : prayer and reflection texts for Christian reconciliation and unity / Bernard de Margerie, author and editor

ISBN 978-0-9920011-1-7 (pbk.)

    1. Ecumenical movement — Prayers and devotions. 2. Liturgics and Christian union. 3. Church — Unity. I. Catholic Church. Diocese of Saskatoon, issuing body II. Bolen, Donald, writer of preface. III. Title.

BX9.5.L55D42 2014   262.001'1   C2014-903560-8

Designed and typeset by Donald Ward.
Cover design by Donald Ward.
Dove sketch by Megan Nobes, United Kingdom, used with permission.
Icon on front cover: Christ the Saviour, Chilandari Serbian Orthodox Monastery, Mount Athos, c. 1360-70.
Printed and bound in Canada.

The Roman Catholic Diocese of Saskatoon
123 Nelson Road
Saskatoon, Saskatchewan, Canada s7s 1H1
www.saskatoonrcdiocese.com

CONTENTS

PART TWO
Christian Communities Praying with and for Each Other

PART THREE
Denominational Voices at Prayer

Universal Prayers

PART FOUR
Resource Texts: Food for discernment

PART FIVE
Gathered Together: Ecumenical Prayer Services
for Christian Reconciliation and Unity

+

DOXOLOGY

We agree ... that the unity we seek
must be unambiguously visible
"so that the world may believe" (John 17:21).
Unity must be recognizable as unity
without an extensive theological gloss.
One must be able to see that the church,
in its ordinary life and practice,
is one community reconciled in Christ.

— from *In One Body Through the Cross*,
The Princeton Proposal for Christian Unity
n. 45, 2003

DEDICATION

This labour of conscience is dedicated to all faithful workers in the vineyard of the reconciliation and healed unity of Christ's disciples, at home in Saskatoon (Canada), and far abroad. It is offered in praise of God's reconciling grace, which covers the earth and the heavens, for ever and ever.

ENDORSEMENT

It is with genuine satisfaction that we, Local Church Leaders in Saskatoon (Canada) and region, grant our collective and public endorsement to the book *In God's Reconciling Grace*, written and edited by Bernard de Margerie, a Roman Catholic priest in Saskatoon. The Church cannot but rejoice and give praise to God for such a newly-fashioned instrument, born on the Vine which is Christ and from the rich and varied traditions of the churches — an aid to prayer and reflection which was until now sorely lacking. We invite a generously wide distribution and congregational/parish use of this book. "Now to him who by the power at work within us is able to accomplish far more than all we can ask or imagine, to him be glory in the church and in Christ Jesus to all generations, forever and ever. Amen." (Ephesians 3:20-21)

+Bryan Bayda, CSsR, Bishop
Ukrainian Catholic Eparchy of Saskatoon

+Donald Bolen, Bishop
Roman Catholic Diocese of Saskatoon

Jeremiah Buhler, Area Church Minister
Mennonite Church Saskatchewan

Rev. Amanda Currie, Clerk
Presbytery of Northern Saskatchewan
The Presbyterian Church in Canada

Rev. Claire Ewert Fisher, Executive Director
Mennonite Central Committee Saskatchewan

+Cynthia G. Halmarson, Bishop
Saskatchewan Synod, Evangelical Lutheran Church in Canada

+David M. Irving, Bishop
Anglican Diocese of Saskatoon

Pastor Brad Mayer
Saskatoon Evangelical Ministers' Fellowship

Rev. Michael Webster, River Bend Presbytery
United Church of Canada

March 6, 2014

The author hopes for possible future endorsement and reception
in and by churches, ecclesial communities, denominations, and/or
ecumenical agencies, across the anglophone world.

Bernard de Margerie
jumeau@shaw.ca

ACKNOWLEDGEMENTS

MY WHOLEHEARTED GRATITUDE GOES, first of all, to my ecumenical Editorial Committee — Bishop Don Bolen, my bishop, whose endorsement and active cooperation were essential to the project, Sandra Beardsall, Amanda Currie, Nick Jesson, and Gertrude Rompré — without whose friendship, sustaining presence, generous and competent assistance this book would not, in the end, have seen the light.

My sincere thanks: to all contributors to this book — some who wrote prayer texts, ecclesially faithful and prophetic; others who pointed to excellent available resources;

to various church communities and agencies who offered, or gave permission to use, various prayer or reflection texts which substantially enriched my own;

to friends and colleagues in the ecumenical community in Saskatoon, relationships which in some cases go back 30, 40, or 50 years;

to the Local Leaders of various Churches, in Saskatoon and region, who gave earnest endorsement to this writing;

to the Prairie Centre for Ecumenism in Saskatoon, to its present Director and staff, as well as directors and staff of years and decades past;

to the Roman Catholic Diocese of Saskatoon, including the faithful who contributed financially to defray production costs of this book;

to Donald Ward, who most competently and generously shaped the manuscript's layout unto printing;

to Sr. Alice LeStrat and Monique Sirois of Sts-Martyrs-Canadiens Roman Catholic parish in Saskatoon: Sr. Alice for her constant friendship and concrete support, Monique for her dedicated support and very much needed and generous word processing expertise;

and most of all, to so many who offered prayer, that this writing be carried out in the holy will of Christ, Lord of his Body, the Church, and still pray faithfully in communion with the aims of these texts;

to all family, faithful friends, parishioners . . .

All is grace!

PREFACE

CHRISTIAN DISCIPLESHIP SUMMONS US to be faithful to the God who is always faithful to us. It invites us to desire what God desires, and to allow our lives to be fashioned by that desire. The Gospel of John tells us something of what God desires when it relates how the night before Jesus died, he prayed to the Father that his disciples would be one, that they would be one just as he is one with the Father. That is a unity which is profound beyond human imagining, yet it is what God desires for us, a complete communion of mind, heart and soul. It is a unity that only God can give.

This volume, *In God's Reconciling Grace*, is intended as an instrument by which we can unite ourselves to God's great desire that we be one.

In his introduction to this volume, Fr. Bernard de Margerie relates that it was on January 25, 1959, the day that Pope John XXIII announced the Second Vatican Council and identified the search for Christian unity as one of its major goals, that his ecumenical vocation was born. He was a newly ordained priest, and was deeply stirred by the notion that Jesus willed that his disciples would be one, and the conviction that the Holy Spirit was actively at work in the Christian churches summoning them to reconciliation and unity.

Over 55 years later, we can say that the stirring Bernard felt that day went deep, because it has lasted, and has nourished a priestly life at the service of reconciliation. In preaching and teaching about Christian unity, in building relations with Christians of diverse Christian communities, in founding the Prairie Centre for Ecumenism, and in a persevering commitment to pray for the unity Christ wills, he has been a pioneer who has reminded us that faithfulness to Christ impels us to seek and to pray for reconciliation among Christians.

The Second Vatican Council's *Decree on Ecumenism*, which brought Pope John's aspirations to fulfilment by launching the Catholic Church into the ecumenical movement, identified spiritual ecumenism as the heart of the search for Christian unity; by this is meant a change of heart, holiness of life, and both public and private prayer for the unity of Christians (UR 8). "Those who identify deeply with Christ must identify with his prayer, and especially with his prayer for unity" (Ecumenical Directory, 25).

Every effort to foster unity among Christians has its roots here. Prayer is essential to authentic dialogue between Christians, foundational to building spiritual bonds of affection, vital to our efforts to give common witness and engage in a common mission. Unity is the work of God in Christ through the Holy Spirit, yet God entrusts us with a share in this work, and a vital part of this work is prayer for unity. It is to be preoccupied with what God is preoccupied with, to yearn for what God yearns for.

In the slow healing of divisions, Christian communities are called to walk with and carry each other, in times of celebration and amidst difficulties and disappointments; and they can only walk this journey together upheld by prayer and centred on the crucified and risen Lord.

It is my hope and conviction that this volume will be a useful tool at the service of that slow healing of divisions. It fills a void, in that our churches are sorely lacking in resources for praying together as Christians. May it find its way to local congregations and individual Christians at the grassroots of the churches. May it be a book of blessing, tilling our hearts, changing our vision, planting in us the great dream of God that we be one, and fashioning us into artisans of reconciliation in the great workshop of the Holy Spirit.

+ Donald Bolen
Bishop of Saskatoon (Canada)
Lent 2014

"I ask . . .
that they may all be one, . . .
so that the world may believe
that you have sent me."

John 17: 20-21

INTRODUCTION

THIS BOOK OF PRAYER TEXTS and other resources is born out of
55 years of ministry in the service of Christian reconciliation and
unity. I received the call to this ministry on January 25, 1959 as
Pope John XXIII announced he was convening a general council
of the Roman Catholic Church. One of the larger purposes of
the Council (that came to be known as Vatican II) was to set the
Catholic Church on a radically new ecumenical course, in renewed
faithfulness to the will and prayer of Christ.

I am not a born writer, and English is not my first language.
I write as a Christian pastor and a minister of Christ in service
to the unity of his Body, the Church. In this book some of the
texts are mine. Others I have gleaned and edited from many and
varied sources. During my years of ministry I came to realize that
there did not exist, in the churches, an instrument or prayer-aid
to assist people in the pew to meditate and pray in earnest so that
Christians and Christian churches would become more obedient
in overcoming their divisions. This writing is an effort to fill that
glaring gap.

It will hopefully be offered and placed in the hands of the
Christian people, at the grassroots, across denominational lines, on
a generously wide basis. It is offered especially as a humble gift and
instrument to those who are called, or may be called in the future,
to spend themselves in this singular act of ecclesial faithfulness:
committed prayer and intercession for the healing of the Body of
Christ.

There are five sections in this book:

Part One *Prayer Matters.* A set of prayer and meditation forms, to introduce readers to ecumenical prayer, and to its many dimensions and implications, its claim to faithfulness.

Part Two *Christian Communities Praying with and for Each Other.* Sketching first steps for parishes/local congregations/other grouping to prayer between denominations

Part Three *Denominational Voices at Prayer.* Hearing the prayer of various Christian traditions (Orthodox, Anglican, Protestant, Roman Catholic, etc.) aimed at Christian unity.

Part Four *Resource Texts: Food for discernment.* Mulling over the foundations of the movement toward Christian reconciliation and unity.

Part Five *Gathered Together: Ecumenical Prayer Services for Christian Reconciliation and Unity.* "Where two or three are gathered in my name, there I am in their midst"

As always, "the Spirit helps us in our weakness; for we do not know how to pray as we ought . . . And God, who searches the heart, knows what is the mind of the Spirit, because the Spirit intercedes for the saints according to the will of God" (Acts 8: 26-27).

The favourable time, the time of grace, is now!

Bernard de Margerie
Saskatoon, SK Canada
Lent 2014

PART ONE

PRAYER MATTERS

"one Lord,
one faith, one baptism,
one God and father of all"

Ephesians 4: 5-6

INTRODUCTION

THE PURPOSE OF THESE PRAYER TEXTS is to assist and encourage Christians to start praying, or pray more often, for the reconciliation and visible unity of Christians.

The prayer of Christ, "that they may all be one, Father, as you are in me and I am in you" (John 17: 21-23), becomes for us an imperative corresponding to the deep desire of his heart. It also invites us to interior conversion.

The Father draws us to the Son; the incarnate Son invites us to follow him on his way of faithfulness on earth, and the Holy Spirit deepens within us the desire that divisions among the disciples of Christ might finally be overcome, for the glory of God and the salvation of the world.

Regarding prayer for unity, we recall the recommendation of the apostle Paul: "pray without ceasing . . . Do not quench the Spirit" (1 Thessalonians 5: 17-19).

These short texts may be used in different ways: they may be added to morning or evening prayer, or at the end of a scripture reading and meditation. They may be used after communion, at eucharist, or again during a time of silence in a liturgy of the Word. The texts are easy to use, and free-standing. They may lead to meditation.

Thus we provide the Christian faithful with a specific everyday tool-for-prayer that has been sorely lacking until now. May the Holy Spirit come and pray in and with us (cf. Romans 8: 26-27), Christ's prayer for the grace-filled unity of his Body . . . Come, Lord Jesus!

1. The Prayer of Christ

foundations

Source   Jesus prayed: "I ask not only on behalf of these, but also on behalf of those who will believe in me through their word, that they may all be one. As you, Father, are in me and I am in you, may they also be in us, so that the world may believe that you have sent me" (John 17: 20-21).

Reflection   The prayer of Christ, our one Lord, Redeemer and Master, speaks to every one in the same way, both in the East and in the West. That prayer becomes an imperative to leave behind our divisions in order to seek and re-establish unity, as a result also of the bitter experiences of division itself (John Paul II, *On Commitment to Ecumenism* n. 65b).

Question   How do I care for Christian unity?

Prayer   Lord Jesus, help me to make my own, your prayer for the unity of your followers — and let this prayer be costly to me. Amen.

           (may be repeated several times during the day)

Reflect . . . pray . . .

2. Kindling the Desire

call to respond

Focus   To be present to Christ, the Lord of ages, Lord of the Church, and pray that the *desire* for Christian reconciliation and unity would grow within me.

Source   I ask not only on behalf of these, but also on behalf of those who will believe in me through their word, that thy may all be one. As you, Father, are in me and I am in you, may they also be in us, so that the world may believe that you have sent me (John 17: 20-21).

Reflection   "To believe in Christ means to desire unity; to desire unity means to desire the Church; to desire the Church means to desire the communion of grace which corresponds to the Father's plan from all eternity. Such is the meaning of Christ's prayer: 'Ut unum sint'" (John Paul II, Encyclical letter on *The Commitment to Ecumenism*, 1995, nn. 9b and 10). Let me take to heart the wounds of division in the Body of Christ (i.e. estrangement, hostility, prejudices, slanders (!), disassociation, verbal violence etc.), and become faithful to the disciplines of prayer, self-offering and suffering if need be, for the healing of those wounds.

Question   What does my conscience tell me here?

Prayer   Lord Jesus, show me how to be more faithful to your will and your prayer for Christian reconciliation and unity. O Holy Spirit, kindle in me the fire of your love! Amen.
(may be repeated several times during the day)

Reflect . . . pray . . .

3. Care for the Body of Christ

faithful response

Source   I, therefore, the prisoner of the Lord, beg you to lead a life worthy of the calling to which you have been called, with all humility and gentleness, with patience, bearing with one another in love, making every effort to maintain the unity of the Spirit in the bond of peace (Ephesians 4: 1-3).

Reflection I will care about Christian unity only if and when my religion goes beyond "Jesus and me." Jesus calls me to expand my heart to care for his Body, the Church — to care for the kingdom of God's love spreading across the world.

Question Can I love Christ without truly loving and caring for his people?

Prayer   O Holy Spirit of God, wholly three, wholly one, stretch my faith and love to include all Christian churches and their members. Amen.
(may be repeated several times during the day)

Reflect ... pray ...

4. God's Plan

Source   He (the high priest) did not say this on his own, but being high priest that year he prophesied that Jesus was about to die for the nation, and not for the nation only, but to gather into one the dispersed children of God (John 11: 51-52).

Reflection   It is the will of God that the whole of humankind, so often and so violently divided, be transformed and become one. For this reason he sent his Son, so that, by dying and rising for all, he might tear down walls of hostility . . .

Question   How can I help to bring different people together?

Prayer   Abba, God, may your will for unity be done on earth as in heaven. Amen.
(may be repeated several times during the day)

Reflect . . . pray . . .

5. Divisions are Hurtful

foundations

Source   Now I appeal to you, brothers and sisters, by the name of our Lord Jesus Christ, that all of you should be in agreement and that there should be no division among you, but that you should be united in the same mind and the same purpose. For it has been reported to me . . . that there are quarrels among you, my brothers and sisters (1 Corinthians 1: 10-11).

Reflection   Division among Christians and the Churches "openly contradicts the will of Christ, scandalizes the world, and damages that most holy cause, the preaching of the Gospel to every creature" (Vatican II, *Decree on Ecumenism*, n. 1a.).

Question   Have I grown accustomed to divisions between churches, and routinely accepted them?

Prayer   O God, convert my heart, that I may comprehend why and how divisions hurt the Body of Christ, the Church. Amen.
(may be repeated several times during the day)

Reflect . . . pray . . .

6. Shaking Off Indifference

confessing sin

Source   For just as the body is one and has many members, and all the members of the body, though many, are one body, so it is with Christ . . . The eye cannot say to the hand, "I have no need of you,'" nor again the head to the feet, "I have no need of you". . . . If one member suffers, all suffer together with it. . . . Now you are the body of Christ and individually members of it (1 Corinthians 12: 12, 21, 26a, 27).

Reflection   A Christian cannot be indifferent to the will and prayer of Christ for his disciples –of all times, including our own—to be united, to be "one," overcoming estrangement.

Question   When was the last time I had a conversation of faith with someone from another church?

Prayer   O Jesus Christ, Lord of the Church, grant unity to your followers, and help me to accept the cost of it, for the sake of the gospel. Amen.
(may be repeated several times during the day)

Reflect . . . pray . . .

7. Call to Conversion

call to respond

Source   A new heart I will give you, and a new spirit I will
put within you; and I will remove from your body the
heart of stone and give you a heart of flesh. I will put
my spirit within you (Ezekiel 36: 26-27a).

Reflection   There can be no ecumenism worthy of the name
without interior conversion. For it is from newness of
attitudes of mind, from self-denial and unstinted love,
that desires of unity take their rise and develop in a
mature way (Vatican II, *Decree on Ecumenism*, n. 7a).

Question   Where and how do I most need "conversion" in
my attitudes toward fellow-Christians of other
denominations?

Prayer   Grant to me, O God, a heart renewed, re-create in me
your own spirit, Lord. Amen.
(may be repeated several times during the day)

Reflect . . . pray . . .

8. Who's Responsible?

awareness

Source   How can you say to your neighbour, "Friend, let me take out the speck in your eye, when you yourself do not see the log in your own eye?" (Luke 6: 42a).

Reflection   "In this one and only Church of God from its very beginnings there arose certain rifts, which the Apostle strongly censures as damnable. But in subsequent centuries much more serious dissensions appeared and quite large Communities became separated from full communion with the Catholic Church — for which, *often enough, men of both sides were to blame*" (Vatican II, *Decree on Ecumenism*, n. 3a; emphasis added). You and I are not responsible for the great divisions that came about in the distant history of the Church . . . but we are all responsible for the spiritual health and faithfulness of the Church in our time, called to pray and work so that divisions may be overcome.

Question   How can I contribute to the spiritual health of my own church?

Prayer   O Holy Spirit, help me enlarge the tent of my heart. Amen.
(may be repeated several times during the day)

Reflect . . . pray . . .

9. Facing Our Prejudices

foundations

Sources   Let anyone who has an ear listen to what the Spirit is saying to the churches (Revelation 2: 7a.) Be of the same mind, having the same love, being in full accord and of one mind. Do nothing from selfish ambition or conceit, but in humility regard others as better than yourselves (Philippians 2: 2b-3).

Reflection   One of the first tasks in seeking reconciliation and unity among Churches, is to learn to eliminate expressions, judgments, prejudices and actions which do not represent with truth and fairness the situation of fellow-Christians from other churches or communities. "But, above all, for the ways in which our divisions have caused a scandal, and been an obstacle to the preaching of the gospel, we need to ask forgiveness of Christ and of each other" (from the Reformed Churches-Roman Catholic International Dialogue, *Towards Common Understanding of the Church*, 1990, n. 63).

Question   Can I name some prejudices I have against other churches, or against fellow-Christians who belong to them?

Prayer   Lord Jesus, help me to seek to do the truth in love in all my attitudes. Amen.
(*may be repeated several times during the day*)

Reflect . . . pray . . .

10. For the Conversion of the Churches

call to respond

Source   And all the churches will know that I am the one who searches minds and hearts (Revelation 2: 23b). For you say, "I am rich, I have prospered, and I need nothing." You do not realize that you are wretched, pitiable, poor, blind and naked . . . I reprove and discipline those whom I love. Be earnest, therefore, and repent (Revelation 3: 17,19).

Reflection   All Christian churches need some form of "ecclesial" conversion, i.e. conversion *as church*. None of our churches — orthodox, catholic, anglican, protestant, evangelical, etc. — can bypass examining their conscience. How can we, as churches, be more faithful to what Christ, Lord of the Church, requires of us? The church we love, each our own church, is always in need of reform, of conversion . . . since we're all human and sinners.

Question   How can I be very aware of my own church's need for conversion, and honest about it, without condemning or being smug about it?

Prayer   Lord Jesus, help me understand and accept that all churches, including my own, need to grow in holiness and faithfulness. Amen.
(may be repeated several times during the day)

Reflect . . . pray . . .

11. Purification of Memories/Healing of Hearts

spiritual journey

Source   You desire truth in the inward being, therefore teach me wisdom in my secret heart . . . Create in me a clean heart, O God, and put a new and right spirit within me (Psalm 51: 6, 10).

Reflection   Nevertheless, besides the doctrinal differences needing to be resolved, Christians cannot underestimate the burden of *long-standing misgivings* inherited from the past, and of mutual *misunderstandings* and *prejudices. Complacency, indifference* and *insufficient knowledge of one another* often make this situation worse. Consequently, the commitment to ecumenism must be based upon the conversion of hearts and upon prayer, which will also lead to the *necessary purification of past memories.* (Pope John Paul II, *Ut Unum Sint*, n. 2, 1995). Memory of the offense — both in individual persons and in churches — can be infused by humble loving-beyond, by letting go of self-affirmation and self-justification at all cost. The heart is healed through conversion to the heart and mind of Christ. Such is the way of churches journeying to reconciliation and fuller unity.

Question   As churches, as local congregations / parishes, and as individual Christians, how much have we/I confronted the need to let go of hurtful memories due to religion? Did we/I pray?

Prayer   O God of mercy and patient healing, purify your Church, your churches, from hurtful memories against each other, for these lead to paralysis, indifference, lingering mistrust and quiet resentment. May our hearts find lasting conversion in the heart of Christ. May we, gladly and hope-filled, seek to be yoked to him. Thus the churches grow in faithfulness. Amen. *(may be repeated several times during the day)*

Reflect . . . pray . . .

12. Recovering the Joy of the Gospel*

call to respond

Source (n. 10) The Gospel offers us the chance to live life on a higher plane, but with no less intensity: "Life grows by being given away, and it weakens in isolation and comfort. Indeed, those who enjoy life most are those who leave security on the shore and become excited by the mission of communicating life to others" (Fifth General Conference of the Latin American and Caribbean Bishops, *Aparecida Document*, 29 June 2007, 360). "Let us recover and deepen our enthusiasm, that delightful and comforting joy of evangelizing, even when it is in tears that we must sow . . . And may the world of our time which is searching, sometimes with anguish, sometimes with hope, be enabled to receive the good news, not from evangelizers who are dejected, discouraged, impatient or anxious, but from ministers of the Gospel whose lives glow with fervor, who have first received the joy of Christ" (Paul VI, Apostolic Exhortation, *Evangelii Nuntiandi*, 8 December 1975), 80.

Reflection This is a profound meditation on what it means to find a mature life, to grow in Christian life, to be(come) an evangelizing church/community of disciples. What captures you the most in this teaching? Why?

Question Would you change or add anything to the last sentence of the Source text quoted above *("And may the world of our time . . . ")*?

---

* Inspired by Pope Francis' letter *Evangelii Gaudium, The Joy of the Gospel,* November 2013.

Prayer   As we grow into a reconciling and uniting community, may it be so, Brother Jesus, may it become so! Amen. *(may be repeated several times during the day)*

Reflect . . . pray . . .

13. "Spiritual" Ecumenism

awareness

Source   For all who are led by the Spirit of God are children
of God. For you did not receive a spirit of slavery
to fall back into fear, but you have received a spirit
of adoption. When we cry 'Abba! Father!' it is that
very Spirit bearing witness with our spirit that we are
children of God (Romans 8: 14-16).

Reflection Spiritual ecumenism includes prayer and conversion of
the heart. It deserves to be regarded as the "soul" of the
whole ecumenical movement. "The work of Christian
unity, then, is profoundly and radically a spiritual one,
i.e., it comes from and is a response to the Holy
Spirit. . . . Spiritual ecumenism implies a clear
consciousness of the sinfulness of division among
Christians. Through spiritual ecumenism we are set
free as communities and as individuals from seeking
to justify our divisions and we are moved to seek a
shared life in a reconciled community" (Disciples of
Christ-Roman Catholic International Commission
for Dialogue, *Aposolicity and Catholicity in the Visible
Unity of the Church*, 1981).

Question   How do I need "conversion of the heart"?

Prayer   God our Father, pour out your grace, that the
ecumenical movement in the Church may be, and
remain, spiritually strong. This I ask, through Christ
our Brother. Amen.
(may be repeated several times during the day)

Reflect . . . pray . . .

14. The Holy Spirit, Creator of Unity

foundations

Source There is one body and one Spirit (Ephesians 4: 4a).
But the Advocate, the Holy Spirit, whom the Father
will send in my name, will teach you everything and
remind you of all that I have said to you (John 14: 26).

Reflection The ecumenical movement is a constant invocation of
the Spirit (Joint Working Group of the World Council
of Churches and the Roman Catholic Church, *Fourth
Report*, 1976, 1a). The prayer of Jesus, "that they may
all be one" (John 17: 21), has become increasingly
important to us, and the cause for much prayer and
repentance still. Nevertheless, we are heartened by the
realization that fresh winds of the Spirit are blowing in
the church universal, and we are waiting expectantly
to see what in the providence of God is yet to come.
Our prayer continues to be: "Come, Holy Spirit!"
(Pentecostal-Roman Catholic Dialogue, *Perspectives on
Koinonia*, Conclusion, 1990).

Question How fervent is my prayer to the Holy Spirit for
Christian reconciliation and unity?

Prayer O Holy Spirit, please help dissolve mistrust and
indifference between the churches, and in my own
heart. Amen.
(may be repeated several times during the day)

Reflect . . . pray . . .

15. The Ways of Prayer

awareness

Source   Likewise the Spirit helps us in our weakness; for we do not know how to pray as we ought, but that very Spirit intercedes with sighs too deep for words. And God, who searches the heart, knows what is the mind of the Spirit (Romans 8: 26-27a). So I say to you, ask, and it will be given to you; search, and you will find; knock, and the door will be opened for you. How much more will the heavenly Father give the Holy Spirit to those who ask him! (Luke 11: 9. 12b).

Reflection   One of the most beautiful fruits of true prayer is that it *changes,* or transforms, *the person who is praying!* One must, nonetheless, persevere in prayer. The apostle Paul assures us that the Holy Spirit helps and guides. The Spirit knows that the unity of the Body of Christ resonates deeply in the heart of God, and it is he, the Holy Spirit, who engraves the prayer of Christ "That they may all be one" (John 17: 21) upon the hearts of the faithful.

Question   How can I grow in prayerfulness for Christian unity?

Prayer   Lord Jesus, who spent nights in prayer, help me imitate your prayerfulness, little by little. Amen.
(may be repeated several times during the day)

Reflect . . . pray . . .

16. Thank God for "the real though imperfect union" Which Already Binds Christians Together

gratefulness

Source　　We declare to you what we have seen and heard so that you also may be in fellowship with us; and truly our fellowship is with the Father, and with his Son Jesus Christ .. . . But if we walk in the light as he himself is in the light, we have fellowship with one another, and the blood of Jesus his Son cleanses us from all sin (1 John 1: 3, 7).

Reflection　　All those who believe in Christ and are baptized are truly brothers and sisters in Christ, members of the same Body of the Lord. Despite serious divisions which are still dividing the churches, Christians remain united in their sharing of great gifts of the Christian life, e.g. we all live by the grace of Christ, nourished by the same written Word of God, share in prayer, in baptism for many of us, etc. Thanks be to God! What unites Christians is more fundamental (and, therefore, more important) than what divides us. The "real though imperfect unity" that binds us together calls for the full visible unity which is still gift and task ahead of us. . . . Come, Holy Spirit!

Question　　How could I best express in my life, and build upon, the fellowship that already unites the disciples of Christ?

Prayer　　O Holy Spirit, please broaden my vision of the wonderful things you do in all Christian churches, and make me grateful. Amen.
(may be repeated several times during the day)

Reflect ... pray ...

17. Our Duty to Give Common Witness

call to respond

Source But you will receive power when the Holy Spirit comes upon you; and you will be my witnesses in Jerusalem, in all Judea and Samaria, and to the ends of the earth (Acts 1: 8).

Reflection People who heard the Christian gospel preached for the first time, in the 19th and 20th century, would say to the missionaries: "If Christ is one, why bother us with the things that divide the churches?" It is for the greater glory of God, first of all, that the churches are called upon to overcome their divisions and grow in full visible fellowship. But it is also, and urgently, so that the churches will soon be able to give the world a common, faithful and credible witness to the gospel of our blessed Lord.

Question What examples do I know of, where the churches are already giving common witness? Where are they not?

Prayer Lord Jesus, grant your Church the required unity, so that churches will be encouraged to give stronger and clearer common witness, in the power of the Holy Spirit. Amen.
(may be repeated several times during the day)

Reflect . . . pray . . .

18. How Do I Deal with My Fears?

awareness

Source   And when he got into the boat, his disciples followed him. A gale arose on the lake. . . . And they went and woke him up, saying, "Lord, save us! We are perishing!" And he said to them, "Why are you afraid, you of little faith?" (Matthew 8: 23, 24a, 25, 26a). There is no fear in love, but perfect love casts out fear (1 John 4: 18).

Reflection   Fear is a poor counselor, says the proverb. The gospel, for its part, reminds us to trust the will and prayer of Christ for the sanctification and the unity of his disciples; to trust, courageously, in the power of the Spirit. It's a bit like a family, seriously divided for a long time, and deciding one day to patch things up. It's normal that people may have fears, that perhaps things won't be quite the same once the family is back together, maybe a change in attitude will be called for, a need to abandon some ideas, a need to widen one's tent.

Question   What fear(s), if any, do I have regarding Christian unity?

Prayer   Lord Jesus, pilot of the ship, please do not allow fear to hinder or paralyze me, but graciously grant me a share in your wisdom and courage. Amen.
(may be repeated several times during the day)

Reflect . . . pray . . . . .

19. "For by grace you have been saved through faith" (Ephesians 2: 8)

foundations

Source   For by grace you have been saved through faith, and this is not your own doing; it is the gift of God (Ephesians 2: 7-8). So if anyone is in Christ, there is a new creation: everything old has passed away; see, everything has become new! (2 Corinthians 5: 17-18).

Reflection   Together we confess: By grace alone, in faith in Christ's saving work and not because of any merit on our part, we are accepted by God and receive the Holy Spirit, who renews our hearts while equipping and calling us to good works" (Lutheran World Federation and the Catholic Church, *Joint Declaration on the Doctrine of Justification*, 1999, n. 15, annex 1.2).

Question   How does this fundamental statement sit with you? What prayer rises in your heart?

Prayer   We give you thanks, O God, for this agreement between churches on the doctrine of justification by faith. We ask that you may grant the Christian churches, and their leaders, the grace of perseverance on the journey toward that visible unity which is Christ's will. Amen.
(may be repeated several times during the day)

Reflect . . . pray . . .

20. Giving Thanks for our Common Baptism

foundations

Source   There is one body and one Spirit, just as you were called to the one hope of your calling, one Lord, one faith, one baptism, one God and Father of all, who is above all and through all and in all (Ephesians 4: 4-6). For in the one Spirit we were all baptized into one body — Jews or Greeks, slaves or free — and we were all made to drink of the one Spirit (1 Corinthians 12, 13).

Reflection The apostle Paul names baptism among the great gifts of God upon which is founded the Christian community: one body, one Spirit, one hope, etc. We certainly did not deserve these gifts, these foundations. They flow from God's radical love for humankind, and lead us into Christ, to life eternal. There is but one baptism, one only sacramental immersion of grace in Christ. Let us give humble thanks to God.

Question   Do you have relatives and/or friends who have been baptized in churches other than your own? Think about those persons; give thanks to God for their baptism.

Prayer   O Christ, grant us, in your love, that the Churches might recover their visible unity in the one and only baptism in which their members are incorporated to you. Amen. (drawn from *The Lima Liturgy* intercession)
(may be repeated several times during the day)

Reflect . . . pray . . .

21. Truly Sisters and Brothers in Christ

foundations

Source But to the one who had told him this, Jesus replied, "Who is my mother, and who are my brothers?" And pointing to his disciples, he said, "Here are my mother and my brothers! For whoever does the will of my Father in heaven is my brother and sister and mother" (Matthew 12: 48-50). As many of you as were baptized into Christ have clothed yourselves with Christ . . . for all of you are one in Christ Jesus (Galatians: 3: 27-28).

Reflection Do I consider the faithful of Christian churches other than my own as my true sisters and brothers in Christ? This is a fundamental fact of our faith, not a pious wish. We are joined with Christ, and to each other, by the one baptism which gives rise to our common life in the Lord. Christ gives us to each other, he entrusts us to each other's care.

Question How do you train your mind to consider "other" Christians as your true relatives in Christ?

Prayer Lord Jesus, help me to remember constantly how your grace, signified and given in the one baptism, consecrates us as sisters and brothers in you. Kindle in us the desire to live worthily in such fellowship, on the basis of faith itself. Amen.
(may be repeated several times during the day)

Reflect . . . pray . . .

22. Prayer as Examination of Conscience

call to respond

Source   O Lord, you have searched me and known me. You know when I sit down and when I rise up; you discern my thoughts from far away. You search out my path and my lying down, and are acquainted with all my ways (Psalm 139: 1-3). Create in me a clean heart, O God, and put a new and right spirit within me (Psalm 51: 12).

Reflection   It is through a praying heart ("go into your room and shut the door and pray to your Father who is in secret," Matthew 6: 6) that Jesus can speak to his disciple, and lead him/her to an examination of conscience. How faithful am I to the gospel? To the community of believers? The Lord also speaks to his Church, and the churches, asking them to examine their ecclesial conscience.

Question   How could my attitudes toward "other" Christians, become more Christian themselves?

Prayer   Lord Jesus, guide us by the inspiration of the Spirit to a genuine examination of conscience, both as individuals and as churches. May we acknowledge sins of blindness, pride, self-satisfaction, and indifference. May we receive from you the grace of true conversion. Amen.
(may be repeated several times during the day)

Reflect . . . pray . . .

23. "Mary: Grace and Hope in Christ"[*]

call to respond

Source   When Elizabeth heard Mary's greeting, the child leapt in her womb. And Elizabeth was filled with the Holy Spirit and exclaimed with a loud cry. . . . Blessed is she who believed that there would be a fulfilment of what was spoken to her by the Lord. And Mary said, "My soul magnifies the Lord, and my spirit rejoices in God my saviour, for he has looked with favour on the lowliness of his servant" (Luke 1: 41-42, 45-48).

Reflection   Recently, some churches — Anglican, Catholic, Protestant — have begun to dialogue on the role of Mary, the mother of the Lord, in the divine plan of salvation in Jesus Christ, and thus also, on the place of devotion to Mary among the Christian faithful: "Our hope is that, as we share in the one Spirit by which Mary was prepared and sanctified for her unique vocation, we may together participate with her and all the saints in the unending praise of God (*Mary: Grace and Hope in Christ*, n. 80, conclusion).

Question   Do I have a devotion to Mary, the Mother of Jesus? Why or why not?

---

[*]   This is the title of an ecumenical document published in 2005 (also called The Seattle Document) by the Anglican-Roman Catholic International Commission.

Prayer   May the mystery of Mary "full of grace" inspire all your disciples, Lord Jesus, to follow you faithfully on the way to the kingdom, and may her prayer help us to overcome our divisions. Amen.
(may be repeated several times during the day)

Reflect . . . pray . . .

24. That the Churches Might Help Carry Each Other's Burdens

call to respond

Source   Bear one another's burdens, and in this way you will fulfil the law of Christ (Galatians 6: 2). So if I, your Lord and Teacher, have washed your feet, you also ought to wash one another's feet. For I have set you an example, that you also should do as I have done to you (John 13: 14-15).

Reflection   Jesus did warn us: "By this everyone will know that you are my disciples, if you have love for one another" (John 13: 35). If I profess to be a Christian, it follows that as a member of a given church, I must stand ready to share the pain, worries and trials of another church, inasmuch as possible. I am duty bound to pray sincerely for that church, and show honest and clear solidarity.

Question   Think about some difficulties faced by other churches at the present time that you could "carry" in prayer . . .

Prayer   O God, who loves us as a beloved Mother and Father, strengthen the churches, and individual Christians, that they may learn to carry each other's burdens in these difficult times. We ask this in faithfulness to your Son, Jesus Christ, in the communion of the Holy Spirit. Amen.
(may be repeated several times during the day)

Reflect . . . pray . . .

25. The "Invisible Monastery"

faithful response

Source   Therefore, as the Holy Spirit says, "Today, if you hear his voice, do not harden your hearts" . . . but exhort one another every day, as long as it is called "today" (Hebrews 3: 7-8a, 13a).

Reflection   Father Paul Couturier (d. 1953), the pioneer apostle of Christian Unity in France, is the one who coined and promoted the concept of the "Invisible Monastery." By this term, he meant the monastery "made up of all the souls which, across the entire world, pray for Unity." He also invited Christians "to join in a holy and fraternal emulation of humble and penitent prayer, of the deepening of one's interior life" (see *L'oecuménisme spirituel de Paul Couturier aux défis actuels*, Profac 2002, p. 133). The invisible monastery, surely the work of the Spirit, is calling again *today* for vocations to on-going steadfast prayer for unity.

Question   What is the gospel reason for the existence of the "invisible monastery"? Am I called to become part of it, in my corner of the world?

Prayer   Come, Holy Spirit! Fill and fortify the hearts of your faithful. May they burn with the fire of your love, and unite themselves fervently to the prayer of Jesus for the full visible unity of his Church. Amen.
(may be repeated several times during the day)

Reflect . . . pray . . .

26. Christ, the One Foundation of the Church[*]

confessing sin

Source   According to the grace of God given to me, like a skilled master builder I laid a foundation, and someone else is building on it. Each builder must choose with care how to build on it. For no one can lay any foundation other than the one that has been laid; that foundation is Jesus Christ (1 Corinthians 3: 10-11).

Confession and pardon (*with two voices, if warranted*)

V 1   O Christ, you are peace and reconciliation!

V 2   Forgive us for often choosing jealousy and animosity rather than confidence and respect between churches. (*moment of silence*)

V 1   O Christ, you give us an abundance of blessings in the unity of faith!

V 2   Forgive us for often choosing isolation and refusing to be a blessing for each other between churches. (*moment of silence*)

V 1   O Christ, you have given joy to the afflicted, liberation to the captives, pardon to sinners!

V 2   Forgive us for having closed our hands and turned our faces away from those who need help. (*moment of silence*)

---

[*] Based on the Ecumenical Prayer Service proposed for the Week of Prayer for Christian Unity, 2005.

V 1	O Christ, you have gathered us together as a shepherd gathers his flock and then goes to seek the one sheep that is lost!
V 2	Forgive us for having often strayed far from you, and pushed you away, thus underlining our divisions. (*moment of silence*)

Prayer for forgiveness

Gracious God, no one can lay any foundation other than the one that has been laid. That foundation is Jesus Christ. We admit that we have not been able to finish building on this foundation in such a way that we may become the dwelling place of God. We have sometimes even been the cause of its ruin. Even if our work should be lost, save us, Lord, and give us a fresh chance to work for unity. Create in us an ardent longing for the unity of your Church and enable us to work towards it. Amen.

27. "For where two or three are gathered in my name, I am there among them" (Matthew 18: 20)*

call to respond

Source   For where two or three are gathered in my name, I am there among them (Matthew 18: 20).

Reflection This verse was the theme proposed for the Week of Prayer for Unity 2006: "The thinking behind this is to encourage and strengthen the fellowship of God's people *in small communities* as well as in great gatherings, in daily life as well as in official, liturgical celebrations. Faithfulness to God's call is not limited to large assemblies, but involves coming together in love, prayer and bible study by *"two or three"* in the name of Jesus. In fact, it is the lives of individuals united in mutual love which brings about the kingdom of God on earth (from the introduction; emphasis added).

Question   How could you take part in, and encourage the formation of small ecumenical groups in your area?

---

* Excerpted from the Ecumenical Prayer Service proposed for the Week of Prayer for Christian Unity, 2006.

Prayer   Lord Jesus Christ,
You call us together in faith and love.
Breathe again the new life of your Holy Spirit among us,
that we may hear your holy word,
pray in your name,
seek unity among Christians
and live more fully the faith we profess.
All glory and honour be yours
with the Father, and the Holy Spirit, for ever and ever.
Amen.
(may be repeated several times during the day)

Reflect . . . pray . . .

28. Holiness, Way to Unity

foundations

Source   For this reason we have not ceased praying for you and asking that you may be filled with the knowledge of God's will in all spiritual wisdom and understanding, so that you may lead lives worthy of the Lord, fully pleasing to him, as you bear fruit in every good work and as you grow in the knowledge of God (Colossians 1: 9-10).

Reflection The closer we get to Christ, our living Lord, the closer we move toward each other, by the same movement. How does one draw closer to Christ? By deeper trust in him, a willingness to welcome his friendship, to imitate him in our attitudes and behaviours, particularly his compassion and capacity to forgive: "Take my yoke upon you, and learn from me; for I am gentle and humble in heart, and you will find rest for your souls. For my yoke is easy, and my burden is light" (Matthew 11: 29-30).

Question How can we encourage each other, across denominations, to draw closer to Christ, our living Lord?

Prayer   Loving God, the universal presence of saints in our churches shows proof of the transcendence and power of the Holy Spirit. Lead us, we implore you, by the paths of genuine holiness, to the full and visible communion *(koinonia)* of your Church. In the name of Jesus Christ, your Son, our Lord. Amen.
(may be repeated several times during the day)

Reflect . . . pray . . .

29. The Churches in Difficult Times

prayer needed

Source　　As you therefore have received Christ Jesus the Lord, continue to live your lives in him, rooted and built up in him and established in the faith, just as you were taught, abounding in thanksgiving. See to it that no one takes you captive through philosophy and empty deceit (Colossians 2: 6-8a). I am now rejoicing in my sufferings for your sake, and in my flesh I am completing what is lacking in Christ's afflictions for the sake of his body, that is, the church (Colossians 1: 24).

Reflection　It seems obvious that most Christian churches today, if not all, are negotiating very difficult passages, of all kinds — encounter with modernity and secularism, uncertain interpretations of traditional faith, weakening of missionary resolve, abysmal lack of Christian culture — to name a few. From the perspective of unity, churches are suffering either by their own indifference to the issue, or because of uncertainties and tensions brought about by the painful lack of unanimity among the churches regarding the unity Christ wills for his Church, and the necessary means to get there.

Question　How do you and your local community live through the present-day trials in the life of the churches?

Prayer   Lord Jesus, you see the wave of pain and powerlessness sweeping over the churches in our time. May the Father and you deign to send anew your Spirit of holiness and spiritual power; may your Spirit come again over the church, consoling us in the sufferings that assail us, and renewing us to be more courageously faithful. Amen.
(may be repeated several times during the day)

Reflect . . . pray . . .

30. Praying for Other Churches

prayer needed

Source   So the churches were strengthened in the faith and increased in numbers daily (Acts 16: 5). If one member suffers, all suffer together with it; if one member is honoured, all rejoice together with it. Now you are the body of Christ and individually members of it (1 Corinthians 12: 26-27). All the churches of Christ greet you (Romans 16: 16b).

Reflection   Many of us have relatives or friends who belong to another church. Perhaps in our own marriage, the two of us belong to two different churches. It is good and proper to pray for other churches, for their welfare and needs. Such prayer will be humble, moved by sincere charity.

Question   Why and how have you (ever) prayed for other churches?

Prayer   O Christ Jesus, head of the Church, please teach me how to pray sincerely for the other churches, according to your wisdom and the desires of your heart. Holy Spirit, please pray this prayer within me, and assist me in my great weakness. Amen.
(may be repeated several times during the day)

Reflect . . . pray . . .

31. To Serve Humankind Together

call to respond

Source But a Samaritan while travelling came near him; and when he saw him, he was moved with pity. He went to him and bandaged his wounds, having poured oil and wine on them. Then he put him on his own animal, brought him to an inn, and took care of him (Luke 10: 33-34). For the creation waits with eager longing for the revealing of the children of God. . . . We know that the whole creation has been groaning in labour pains until now (Romans 8: 19, 22).

Reflection The world that "God so loved" is scarred with problems and tragedies which cry out for the compassionate engagements of Christians (from *The Church: Towards a Common Vision*, n. 64). When churches work together for social justice and sound social development, they give credible witness to Christ the Servant, and show the unity already existing among them.

Question How many projects can you think of that churches carry out together in the service of the poor in your area?

Prayer Holy God, be a light to the churches and guide them on the path of common service in the cause of justice, compassion and peace, for the sake of the human community for which you offered your own witness and life. Amen.
(may be repeated several times during the day)

Reflect . . . pray . . .

32. Unity in Diversity

call to respond

Source So we, who are many, are one body in Christ, and individually we are members one of another. We have gifts that differ according to the grace given to us (Romans 12: 5-6).

Reflection The unity of the Church is a unity-in-diversity, e.g. diversity in the ways the one faith is expressed, diversity in forms of worship, etc. However, in our present situation of churches "divided," diversity often becomes "divisive" if it is not anchored enough on a fundamental unity of church faith and life.

Question Can you think of "diversities" that enhance the unity in churches, and of others that hinder that unity?

Prayer Help your churches, Lord Jesus, to overcome the true divisions that disfigure your one Church; may the churches re-learn, wisely and courageously, the way of genuine unity-in-diversity, by the grace of the Holy Spirit. Amen.
(may be repeated several times during the day)

Reflect . . . pray . . .

33. "In One Body through the Cross"[*]
(Ephesians 2:16)

call to respond

Source   So we are ambassadors for Christ, since God is making his appeal through us; we entreat you on behalf of Christ, be reconciled to God (2 Corinthians 5: 20).

Reflection The journey toward full communion requires a disciplined effort on the part of the churches. This discipline-for-unity is at the heart of the Christian vocation. It is and will be a costly discipline. Yet we must hold, in hope, that any true step toward unity will bear new life in Christ, he who reconciles us — in one body through the cross.

Question How do you understand "costly" grace? Does God offer his people grace that costs a lot? How?

Prayer Lord Jesus, head of the Church, your body, please grant the churches, their leaders and members the courage to accept and embrace the efforts required to commit to full *koinonia*, you who reconcile us by means of the cross, in the power of the Holy Spirit. Amen.
(may be repeated several times during the day)

Reflect . . . pray . . .

---

[*] Inspired by the ecumenical text *In One Body Through the Cross* — The Princeton Proposal for Christian Unity, 2003.

PART TWO

CHRISTIAN COMMUNITIES PRAYING WITH AND FOR EACH OTHER

"Let the same mind
be in you
that was in Christ Jesus"

Philippians 2: 5

INTRODUCTION

THE PRAYER TEXTS IN THIS SECTION are intended to help Christians and congregations/parishes undertake the long faithful journey of embracing Christian denominations *other* than their own in prayer imbued with sisterly/brotherly love and solidarity. Such a journey needs to be learned. The expansion of one's prayer horizon does not, unfortunately, come spontaneously. It needs to be learned as a new spiritual discipline. The Holy Spirit teaches us, little by little, this enlarged prayer as an act of humble solidarity with the whole Church, the whole Body of Christ.

We know that true prayer is an act and a school of discipleship. In the exercise of prayer for Christian reconciliation and unity, Christ teaches us to share in his own heart and mind, in his own prayerfulness. The very act of yielding to him in prayer bends the heart to new obedience. In and through prayer, dis-unity begins to melt and heal. We learn a spirit of humility purifying us of arrogance. Fear subsides. We step out of our self-centeredness, personal and/or denominational. We learn to let antagonistic prejudice die, to forego murderous indifference and to take on the burdens of "other" Christians, within Christ's compassion. In the teaching of Philippians 2: 3-5: "Do nothing from selfish ambition or conceit, but in humility regard others as better than yourselves. Let each of you look not to your own interests, but to the interests of others. Let the same mind be in you that was in Christ Jesus."

The next few pages represent a *beginning* in the expansive and profound spirituality of "Christian communities at prayer with and for each other." Much more will be added as churches learn and grow in this manner of being-together, as we journey in obedience towards more healing, more shared energy for mission, a deeper unity, more faithfulness. "There can be no ecumenism worthy of the name without interior conversion" (Vatican II, *Decree on Ecumenism*, n. 7). Personal conversion. Denominational conversion. God rejoices in adoration and praise rising from desires, prayer, and action fostering unity.

The following prayer texts can be used in several ways: as part of Sunday worship, printed in the Sunday Service bulletins, individually, in small groups, etc. Let us not stop praying.

1. Litany for all Christian churches or ecclesial communities

(after each invocation, the invited response is
**Forgive our divisions, O God, heal our wounds,
grant us faithfulness!**)

- For the Eastern and Oriental Orthodox Churches, we pray:
  Forgive. . .
- For the Roman and Eastern Catholic Churches, we pray:
  Forgive. . .
- For the Lutheran, Anabaptist and Reformed Churches, we pray:
  . . .
- For the Anglican and Old Catholic Churches, we pray: . . .
- For the Baptist, Evangelical, and other Free Churches, we pray:
  . . .
- For the Methodist, Holiness, and Pentecostal Churches, we
  pray: . . .
- For the United, Disciples, and all Union Churches, we pray: . . .
- For the thousands of independent, indigenous congregations,
  we pray: . . .

Lamb of God, you take away the sins of the world,
have mercy on us. AMEN.

2. Several denominations praying together — on the local, regional, or worldwide levels

God, we praise you for the real though imperfect communion
that joins our churches together.
We praise you, we bless you, we adore you, we glorify you,
we give you thanks for your great glory!
— And we beg your forgiveness for our sins
against the blood and the Body of Christ
— for, so often, we do not know what we are doing.
"Grant to us, O Lord, a heart renewed,
re-create in us your own Spirit, Lord."
This we pray, through Christ our Lord. AMEN.

(refrain drawn from Jeremiah and Ezekiel)

3. Praying for another Christian denomination

Lord Jesus, we pray for the N . . . (name of church, denomination or
tradition) throughout the world.
We rejoice and give you thanks for the real though imperfect unity
that joins us together.
From within the whole Body of Christ,
we pray that these sisters and brothers of ours
may grow in faithfulness to the gospel:
in the clear joy of charity, in pure, strong and peaceful witness,
in the inner cohesion of its members — faithful and leaders
together —
according to your holy will and grace.
And as we pray for them,
we humbly ask for the kindness of their prayer for us.
In your name we pray, Lord Jesus. AMEN.

4. Ordering mission, life and ministry in the church: accessing the common faith

Help us, O Holy Spirit of Jesus,
in our seemingly intractable divisions.
The Lord Jesus promised that you would lead his disciples
into complete truth (John16: 13),
that you would help us find
the right concepts and words (cf. Luke 11: 11b-12),
to hold fast to, or recover,
and proclaim together the common Christian faith.
Come to us with your recreative power, O Holy Spirit of God,
and lead us in reconciling our seemingly diseased diversities
regarding baptism, the Eucharist or Holy Communion,
ordained ministry and Christ-authority in the one Church.
We make this prayer from the depths of our poverty. AMEN.

5. For a given denomination in a time of particular trial

Lord Jesus, at this time we / I lift to your wounded side on the
cross the N . . . (name of denomination / church).
As you were not spared the way of the cross,
so your Church, your churches, will not be spared
walking in your self-emptying footsteps.
Grant this ecclesial community, our sister church,
to discern and live through this trial yoked to you,
secure in the faith that its life is hidden with you,
O Christ, in God (cf. Colossians 3: 3).
May other Christian churches stand to defend, assist
and console the N's . . .
knowing well by experience that we are all subject
to pruning by God in the true vine which is you,
O faithful, gentle and strong Christ. Come, Lord Jesus! AMEN.

(The next four prayer intentions relate to churches preparing to commemorate, in 2017, the 500th anniversary of the Protestant Reformation. The four texts were inspired by remarks made by Pastor Olaf Tveit, General Secretary of the World Council of Churches, October 13, 2013.)

6. In times of extraordinary trial and hardship in the life of a neighbour or partner congregation

O God, father and mother of all,
our sisters and brothers of N . . . (parish/congregation)
are presently carrying (a) very heavy burden(s).
Your apostle Paul has urged upon us this first principle in Christ: "If one member suffers, all suffer together with it" (1 Corinthians 12: 26).
Help us to resist the sin of indifference,
grant us compassion and steadfast courage to help bandage the wounds of our sisters and brothers in grave need.
Come to their assistance, O God.
Send us, and through us, make haste to help them! AMEN.

7. Repentance

O God of mercy, we humbly ask your forgiveness, and each other's, for the historical events of violence and bloodshed which marred the period of the Lutheran Reformation. We acknowledge that there is genuine historical guilt and blame on all sides.
Father in heaven, please forgive us as we forgive — and not seven times only! Give us the courage and wisdom to be radically mindful of the log in our own eye, rather than focus on the speck in our neighbour's eye (cf. Matthew 7: 1-5).
In the name of Jesus we pray. AMEN.

8. Common reading of the Bible

Beyond the troubled divisions that came in the wake of the
Reformation, we acknowledge, O God, with grateful hearts,
that over the past centuries, and especially during the 20th
century, countless Christians have come together
for a common reading and study of holy Scripture.
Thus the fabric of the Body of Christ
begins to be woven together again and healed.
We give you thanks for this crucial growth in unity
through shared obedience to your Word.
May we live by this Word ever more in undivided faithfulness.
In Jesus' name we pray. AMEN.

9. Martyrs by our hands

Our conscience ponders in sorrow, Lord Jesus,
how many Christians truly became martyrs
through violent persecutions at the hands of fellow-Christians
in the wake of the Reformation.
Help us now, in our churches, as a penitential affirmation,
to begin to carry each other's burdens
across denominational boundaries.
Shed your blinding light, Lord! Have mercy! AMEN.

10. "United in the blood of martyrs"*

O God of strength and mercy,
Father of our Lord Jesus Christ,
we thank you for the *grace of martyrdom* lived out
in your Church along the centuries.
On our journey toward reconciliation and healed unity
between Christian churches and communities,
we recognize with gratitude
the fact that all Christian denominations,
at one time or another, have engendered true martyrs
— those who received from you the strength to shed their blood
in witness to the Christian faith.
Throughout all centuries, including our own,
these sisters and brothers have sought to do the Father's will,
and overcome all obstacles, joining Christ
in the baptism and the cup of his holy death (cf. Mark 10: 38 and
Matthew 20: 21).
Thus, they achieved the perfect communion in God
that still eludes us.
May their unanimous witness spur churches in our day
to do God's will and overcome all obstacles,
in faithful obedience, on our journey towards the reconciliation
and healed unity that Christ wills, by the means that he wills.
AMEN.

---

* Inspired by the letter *On commitment to Ecumenism* (*Ut unum sint*), by Pope
  John Paul II, 1995, nn. 83-84

11. Preparation of the 2017 anniversary

As churches — the Lutheran and Roman Catholic in the first
instance — undertake to commemorate the 500th anniversary of
the beginning of the Reformation,
we ask, O God, that the preparation of this event
be humble, honest, and full of hope.
We make this prayer through Jesus Christ our Lord. AMEN.

12. Parish prayer for openness to the Spirit

O God, we ask you to enlarge the tent of our Christian faith and
witness.
May we be truly open — and converted, if need be —
to respect and care for our sisters and brothers of other Christian
denominations. Please calm our fears, dear God, appease our
denominational jitters,
and dissolve the prejudices we still harbour.
We make this prayer in Jesus' name. AMEN.

13. Prayer between two ecumenical partners

O Lord, we / I pray for the parish/congregation of N . . . ,
our sisters and brothers in Christ.
You have entrusted them to us and we to them
in the charity that builds up your Body.
May you nurture their faithfulness to you on their pilgrim way.
And as we pray for them, we humbly hope that they would do the
same for us.
Through Christ our Lord. AMEN.

*(This prayer text can be adapted for use among several congregations/
parishes.)*

14. Before an ecumenical Bible study

Holy Spirit, come and shed your light upon us.
May our common study of God's holy word
draw us into closer fellowship and obedience within
the Body of Christ, your Son. AMEN.

15. Before joint pastoral meetings between two or several congregations/parishes

O God, the early Christians "devoted themselves
to the apostles' teaching and fellowship,
to the breaking of bread and the prayers" (Acts 2: 42).
Please enlighten and strengthen our faltering steps
as we learn, little by little, to walk together,
give witness and serve together,
despite and through our denominational dividing lines.
Help us to accept the challenging discipline of growth in unity
according to the will and prayer of Jesus.
May we also learn to help carry joyfully each other's burdens
in truth and love. AMEN.

16. Mulling over the demands of social justice in the Gospel, and preparing for a joint (ecumenical) action

Lord Jesus, you were sent to "proclaim release of the captives
and recovery of sight to the blind, to let the oppressed go free" and
"to bring good news to the poor" (Luke 4: 18, cf. Matthew 11, 5).
Thus we know with certainty that the demands of social justice are
an essential part of your gospel.
Help us to hear the cry of the poor — sometimes the cry of whole
peoples, the poorest peoples of the earth.
Grant us, your disciples, to wash our neighbour's feet,
in the various ways called for in today's society,
and here at home.
Teach us to serve and to heal, together and in mutual solidarity,
for you entrust us to each other as you send us out on the pathways
of social justice and compassion.
Be with us, Lord, we pray. AMEN.

17. Preparing for a "dialogue" session — in various contexts

O God of wisdom and mercy,
too much of the life and history of the Church have been marred
by estrangement, misunderstanding and hostility
between disciples of your Son.
May your forgiveness come to us, again and again,
as we strive to repent and forgive one another.
O Holy Spirit, enlighten us and strengthen our mutual trust
and goodwill as we undertake, in dialogue,
to grow in mutual understanding,
and thus hasten steadfastly on the road
of reconciliation and manifest unity.
Grant, O God of mercy, humility,
mutual love, and godly discernment.
We make this prayer through Jesus the Christ,
your Son and our Lord. AMEN.

18. Of Word and Bread
(cf. Luke 24: 23-32)

We beg you, Lord Jesus, patiently draw us together
closer to you and your Way,
by our common faithful meditation on
the Word of God in holy scripture.
If this work of your grace comes back to you
bearing good and lasting fruits of reconciliation and unity,
will not this same grace
lead your unsteady (and often sad, as at Emmaus) disciples
to come together at the table of your self-offered Bread?
How can we truly commune in the one written Word
and not find in our partner-congregation/parish
our spiritual fibre of conviction to do your will?
From our ecclesial weakness,
in doubting hope, we cry out to you, Lord.
God, come to our assistance! Lord, hasten to help us! AMEN.

19. Entering and preparing for Holy Week

Lord Jesus, we know by faith
that the mystery of your saving suffering,
death, resurrection, and sending forth
of the Spirit
is always and forever present and effective
in the midst of your Church and your world.
We also perceive that faith's memory
assists us in responding to your grace, incarnate in human history.
As we (prepare to) enter
in the annual memorial of the entire mystery of Christ,
help us to strengthen and purify our faithfulness,
for the sake of the world you love and save.
Help us not to flee the Cross . . . or the Last Supper. . . ,
or evade the Resurrection . . . through distraction and
lukewarmness.
Open the eyes of our hearts to the courage of giving up
and laying down at the foot of your Mystery
the unholy divisions that separate us from each other,
and prevent us from obeying and yielding to your will and prayer
for the unity of your disciples through the ages.
In our extreme poverty, yet with trusting hope, we pray. AMEN.

20. Entering the Week of Prayer
for Christian Unity

We thank you, dear God, for the inexhaustible grace
you offer the churches of Christ, and their leaders,
in the celebration of the annual
Week of Prayer for Christian Unity.
The unity of the Body is your gift alone,
yet we have neglected, opposed, and wounded
this primordial gift over so many centuries.
In our present poverty and need we humbly and unreservedly
ask for a new and powerful Pentecost of your Spirit, once again
bringing healing and conversion to the churches. May we learn
corrective obedience from your Son:
"who, though in the form of God . . . emptied himself, taking the
form of a slave . . . and . . . humbled himself and became obedient
to the point of death — even death on a cross" (Philippians 2: 6-8).
"Let anyone who has an ear listen to what the Spirit is saying
to the churches" (cf. Revelation 2: 7ff.). AMEN.

21. All denominations: willingness to receive gifts mutually

O Holy Spirit, from the depth of our spiritual poverty we beg you, if it be your will, to enable the Church and the churches
to faithfully *receive* the numerous official and mandated statements produced by various theological dialogue groups over decades of years.
We are open to your surprises, Lord Holy Spirit — come!
Please convert our ecclesial hearts,
so that, earnestly knowing our respective poverties,
we become willing and eager to *receive* true gifts that we need
— from one another, between Christian denominations.
In the name of Jesus we pray. AMEN.

22. All denominations: act of wholehearted thanksgiving

"It is truly right and just, our duty and our salvation,
always and everywhere to give you thanks,
Lord, Holy Father, almighty and eternal God.
For, although you have no need of our praise,
yet our thanksgiving is itself your gift,
since our praises add nothing to your greatness
but profit us for salvation, through Christ our Lord . . .
Holy, Holy, Holy Lord God of Hosts.
Heaven and earth are full of your glory.
Hosanna in the highest.
Blessed is he who comes in the name of the Lord,
Hosanna in the highest." AMEN.

(from the Roman Catholic *Roman Missal*, common Preface IV)

23. A Covenant Prayer*

In the name of God, the Father, Son, and Holy Spirit,
our Creator, Redeemer, and Sustainer,
and in response to the call of Jesus "that they may all be one . . .
so that the world may believe that you have sent me,"
we ask God to enable us, as sisters and brothers in Christ,
to live together in a covenant of Christian love,
understanding, and faithfulness to the Gospel.

We ask God to help us bear faithful witness to the wider Church
and world:

- acknowledging the fractured Body of Christ and the need for
  healing;
- rejoicing in the gift of unity Jesus Christ gives us and
  celebrating the real, though imperfect, communion that we
  share;
- recognizing the value of our respective traditions, and pledging
  to encourage each other to grow in them in a manner that
  unites rather than divides;
- committedly living-out and growing-in the unity that Jesus
  Christ wills for us.

We pray that our covenant with one another
will serve the full communion of the Church as willed by Jesus
Christ, through the empowerment of the Holy Spirit.
And we pray for God's blessing
that we might be faithful to this covenant, to the honour and glory
of God. AMEN.

---

* This prayer text is based upon "A Covenant" between McClure United Church
  and Holy Spirit Roman Catholic Parish, signed March 5, 2000, in Saskatoon,
  Saskatchewan, Canada. This covenant, by the grace of God, continues to be
  lived out by these two communities of Christ's people.

Interreligious (interfaith) awareness — 1

Theme   "Enlarge the site of your tent" (Isaiah 54: 2a)

Source   There is a legitimate and necessary Christian prayer articulated within the community of religions.

"This is right and is acceptable in the sight of God our Saviour, who desires everyone to be saved and to come to the knowledge of the truth. For there is one God; there is also one mediator between God and humankind, Christ Jesus, himself human, who gave himself a ransom for all (1 Timothy 2: 3-6a).

Reflection "The fullness of truth received in Jesus Christ does not give individual Christians the guarantee that they have grasped this truth fully. In the last analysis, truth is not a thing we possess, but a Person by whom we must allow ourselves to be possessed. While keeping their identity intact, Christians must be prepared to learn and receive,from and through others, the positive values of their traditions." (from "Dialogue and Proclamation," in *Interreligious Dialogue,* par. 49, nos. 973, 625 — quoted by Tom Ryan, *Interreligious Prayer,* p. 20.)

Prayer   We pray to you, O God, as Father and Mother of all human beings. Lead us, by your Holy Spirit, to respect and love all people, members of all religions, as sisters and brothers, unconditionally loved by you. We rejoice in knowing by Christian faith that all humans are one being created in your own image. We praise you and we give you thanks! And we make our prayer through Christ, your Word and our Saviour. AMEN.

Reflect . . . pray. . .

Interreligious (interfaith) awareness — 2

Theme   Christian prayer with and for other religions and their faithful.

Source   And Jesus replied, "Who are my mother and my brothers?" And looking at those who sat around him, he said, "Here are my mother and my brothers! Whoever does the will of God is my brother and sister and mother" (Mark 3, 33-35).

Jesus said to her, "Woman, believe me, the hour is coming when you will worship the Father neither on this mountain nor in Jerusalem ... But the hour is coming, and is now here, when the true worshippers will worship the Father in spirit and truth, for the Father seeks such as these to worship him. God is spirit, and those who worship him must worship him in spirit and truth" (John 4, 21. 23-24).

Reflection   "All this (hope in the resurrection) holds true not only for Christians but also for all people of good will in whose hearts grace is active invisibly. For since Christ died for everyone, and since all are in fact called to one and the same destiny, we must hold that the Holy Spirit offers to all the possibility of being made partners, in a way known to God, in the paschal mystery" (Vatican II, *Gaudium et Spes*, Pastoral Constitution on the Church in the Modern World, n. 22).

Prayer   O God of all human beings and of all creation, we dare to pray, however seldom we do so, with and for our sisters and brothers of all religions. We do so trusting in you alone and despite the fragility and defects of our own faith.

May we be granted a change of heart when we realize that our own religion, or its members, behave / have behaved in a wrongful manner. Grant us the humility to recognize our wrongs and the courage to mend our ways — as indeed we all must!

We pray that the faithful of all religions may grow in humanity and in spirituality before you, O God. May we all live more faithfully, constantly caring for all our neighbours, especially the poorest, the most marginalised, the most in need. May we all honour and serve the eminent dignity of each and every human being.

In your Holy Spirit we commit to offer steady good example in matters of faith, godly life, social justice, compassion and peacefulness — for the universal welfare of humankind, in your sight and by your great mercy, O God. In the name of Jesus we pray. AMEN.

Reflect . . . pray. . .

PART THREE

DENOMINATIONAL VOICES AT PRAYER

"All this is from God,
who reconciles us to himself
through Christ,
and has given us
the ministry of reconciliation"

2 Corinthians 5: 18

INTRODUCTION

PART THREE WILL LEAD READERS INTO PRAYER following *in the spiritual footsteps of various Christian denominations or confessions.* The prayer texts are gathered from various denominational sources and issue from the heart of the respective traditions. The sampling of denominational *Voices* represented here, as varied and rich as it is, is nonetheless only a beginning. It limps somewhat and is far from complete. It is not, therefore, a finished product, but opens up to a fuller and stronger development in the future.

Some texts represent the historical, foundational, and traditional stance(s) of given denominations regarding Christian reconciliation and unity.

Other texts represent modern, contemporary voices, again issuing from various denominations and expressing, for today and tomorrow, prayerful thought and best desires toward the healing of divisions in the Body of Christ. They draw from Scripture, and give voice to particular perspectives, questions, repentance, conviction leading into the future.

Christian denominations each have ecclesial gifts and endowments, yet do not existentially embody the fullness of the one Church, Body of Christ. Hence the constant need for conversion of the churches. May all humble and sincere prayer, though imperfect and limited, be overshadowed, purified and lifted up by the Holy Spirit, and serve God's purpose for the one, holy, catholic and apostolic Church of the Lord Jesus, for the sake of the world God loves. Maranatha!

Part Three also includes a brief anthology of prayer texts emanating from the World Council of Churches and the Pontifical Council for the Promotion of Christian Unity (Roman Catholic).

1. From the Anglican Communion

foundational/traditional

For the Church Universal
(Book of Common Prayer)

Most gracious God, we humbly beseech thee for thy holy Catholic Church: Fill it with all truth; in all truth with all peace. Where it is corrupt, purify it; where it is in error, direct it; where anything is amiss, reform it; where it is right, strengthen and confirm it; where it is in want, furnish it; where it is divided and rent asunder, make it whole again; through Jesus Christ our Lord. Amen.

foundational/traditional

For the Unity of all Christian People
(Book of Common Prayer)

O God the Father of our Lord Jesus Christ, our only Savior, the Prince of Peace: Give us grace seriously to lay to heart the great dangers we are in by our unhappy divisions. Take away all enmity and prejudice, and whatsoever else may hinder us from godly union and concord; that as there is but one Body and one Spirit, and one hope of our calling, one Lord, one faith, one baptism, one God and Father of us all, so we may henceforth be all of one heart and of one soul, united in one holy bond of truth and peace, of faith and charity, and may with one mind and one mouth glorify thee; through Jesus Christ our Lord. Amen.

(Reverend Jan Bigland-Pritchard, Saskatoon)

Almighty God, in love you sent your son Jesus Christ who is the way, the truth and the life: Grant to all, who call upon his name in faith, courage to pursue the unity he prayed for, holding fast to the truth he lived; who is alive and reigns with you in the unity of the Holy Spirit, now and forever.   Amen.

contemporary

A Poem
(Gordon Light, born 1944)

Draw the circle wide. Draw it wider still.
Let this be our song, no one stands alone, standing side by side,
draw the circle wide.

God the still-point of the circle, 'round whom all creation turns;
nothing lost, but held forever, in God's gracious arms.

Let our hearts touch far horizons, so encompass great and small;
let our loving know no bounds, faithful to God's call.

Let the dreams we dream be larger, than we've ever dreamed before;
let the dream of Christ be in us, open every door.

2. From the Evangelical Tradition

a) Baptist voice

traditional

Blest Be The Tie That Binds

(Hymn by John Fawcett, Baptist pastor, theologian and hymn writer, 1739-1817)

Blest be the tie that binds our hearts in Christian love:
The fellowship of kindred minds is like to that above.

Before our Father's throne we pour our ardent prayers;
Our fears, our hopes, our aims are one, our comforts and our cares.

We share our mutual woes, our mutual burdens bear;
And often for each other flows the sympathizing tear.

When we asunder part it gives us inward pain;
But we shall still be joined in heart, and hope to meet again.

This glorious hope revives our courage by the way;
While each in expectation lives and longs to see the day.

From sorrow, toil and pain, and sin we shall be free;
And perfect love and friendship reign thru' all eternity.

For Unity And Peace

(Prayer from *Gathering for Worship: Patterns and Prayers for the Community of Disciples*, section "Disciples on the Way: Worship Throughout the Year," Prayer #197, adapted)

Lord Jesus Christ,
you said that you were one with the Father
and you gave your Spirit to the disciples,
offering them your peace;
we pray for the unity of your Church
and the peace of your world.
Lord God, forgive us the fears and suspicions,
the half truths and ignorance which reinforce our divisions.
We pray that your Spirit of truth will open our minds
so that we might learn from one another.
We pray that your Spirit of love will fill our hearts
that we might forgive and encourage one another.
We pray that your Spirit of unity will work in our lives,
binding us together in you,
our only God, Father, Son, and Holy Spirit.
We pray for your world, broken into hostile camps by fear,
hatred, suspicion, greed, and the pursuit of power.
...
We pray that the search for unity in your Church
might serve the search for unity in our divided world.
For there is one God and Father of all,
who is over all, and through all, and in all.

(Reverend Paul Matheson, Saskatoon)

Lord Jesus Christ,
you have called us to be your followers.
Help us to see that we are not alone,
that others, too, have embraced your invitation
to be loving, obedient,
servants of your kingdom in the world.
Forgive us our wilful pride.
Heal the divisions that separate us, one from another.
Help us to value the gifts that each one brings.
Strengthen congregations,
that we may be partners in the healing of creation.
Send your Spirit upon us,
and enable us to live together,
bearing faithful witness to you, O Lord,
to the glory of God, our heavenly Father.
AMEN.

b) Christian and Missionary Alliance voice

affirmation of faith

(Editorial on Christian Alliance Constitution and Founding, 1887)

The Christian Alliance is designed to be a simple and fraternal
union of all who hold in common the fullness of Jesus in His
present grace and His coming glory.
It is not intended in any way to be an engine of division
or antagonism in the churches, but, on the contrary,
to embrace Evangelical Christians of every name
who hold this common faith and life.

Renew Thy Church

(a hymn drawn from *Hymns of the Christian Life*, 1978; author: Kenneth L. Cober, 1902; proposed by Russell Pepler, Saskatoon)

Renew Thy Church, her ministries restore: both to serve and adore.
Make her again as salt through the land, and as light from a stand.
'Mid somber shadows of the night, where greed and hatreds spread
    their blight,
Oh, send us forth with power endued, help us, Lord, to be renewed.

Teach us Thy Word, reveal its truth divine, on our path let it shine;
Tell of Thy works, Thy mighty acts of grace, from each page show
    Thy face.
As thou hast loved us, sent Thy Son, and our salvation now is won.
Oh, let our hearts with love be stirred, help us Lord, know Thy
    Word.

Teach us to pray, for Thou art ever near, Thy still voice let us hear.
Our souls are restless till they rest in Thee, this our glad destiny.
Before Thy presence keep us still that we may find for us Thy will,
And seek Thy guidance every day, teach us Lord, how to pray.

Teach us to love, with strength of heart and mind, everyone, all
    mankind,
Break down old walls of prejudice and hate, leave us not to our fate.
As Thou hast loved and given Thy life to end hostility and strife,
Oh, share Thy grace from heaven above, teach us how to love.

c) Evangelical (at large) voice

contemporary

A Prayer to Christ for Vision
(Dr. Bill Blackmon, Saskatoon)

Forgiving and Loving Christ:
Your words are direct and easy to understand.
Your only recorded prayer
pleads with your Father that Your followers would be one.
Loving one another was your most ardent command.
We have been divided, and in competition, for so long,
that almost none of us
have experienced this desire which burns within you.
Because you prayed it, however, Lord Jesus,
there is no question or doubt —
it will occur!
For those of us who have only seen this burning
in your heart from afar,
Give us visions to carry us further!
Show us what this looks like in your eyes!
Strengthen us with the knowledge of this certainty!
Forgive our willful blindness!
Help us to settle for nothing less —
that they may know You by our love for one another..
Oh ever kind and patient Christ,
Hear our Prayer.
AMEN.

We Stand on the Structure and Labour...

(Dr. Bill Blackmon, Saskatoon)

Eternal Father:
We stand on the structure and labour
of the sowing and planting and harvesting
of the saints of twenty-one centuries
— from all your church — over all the earth.
Forgive our narrow thoughts which consider our moment
the only moment of value.
Remind us that many before us
have carried your heart for Unity and Oneness
long before we had any idea of your desire to bring us together.
Humble us to see that
without these seeds
we would have no plant to water or flower to grow.
Encourage us as you reveal that our little part
— like the widow's mite —
is by your choice vitally important.
We pray this in the mighty Name
of the One who is the Three
— Our Saviour, our Model, our Redeemer.
AMEN.

d) Evangelical/Orthodox voice

contemporary

Prayer for unity

(by Bishop Joshua Beecham, Indianapolis, USA, proposed by Fr. Jakob Palm, Saskatoon)

(a) O Blessed Heavenly Father,
from whom every family in heaven and on earth is named:
Your Only-begotten Son, in the fervent prayer He offered
before His voluntary death, indicated that the world's ability
to believe that you sent Him would be directly related
to the visible unity of Your Church.
Therefore, before we ask you to bless the missionary efforts
of our Particular Christian Traditions,
we earnestly plead that You would restore that unity among all Christians
without which evangelism becomes scandalous.

(b) Grant us humility,
that we may count others as better than ourselves;
hospitality, that, although we have become strangers,
we may welcome each other as brothers and sisters in Christ;
discernment, that we may distinguish orthodox matters of faith
that are binding upon all Christians
from personal or denominational convictions that are not;
courage, that we may work through our differences
with integrity and mercy;
and love, that we may beat our swords into ploughshares,
working together to bring hope to those in despair;
healing, to those who are broken;
deliverance, to those who are bound;
and the light of Your gospel to the whole world.
(c) Forgive us our divisions, O Lord, and heal us,

that by our sincere love for one another
we may be recognized as disciples of Your Son;
that even though some may mock us,
they may see our good deeds done in unity
and glorify You on the day of visitation.
This we ask in the name of Jesus Christ our Lord,
who by His cross has reconciled us to You
and conquered hostility with charity;
who with You and the Holy Spirit lives and reigns,
one God, now and ever and unto ages of ages.
AMEN

e) Mennonite voice

foundational

(A profession of "evangelical faith" by Menno Simons (1496-1561), leader of a branch of the Anabaptists (16th century) who came to be known as Mennonites. This text was proposed by Garth and Claire Ewert Fisher, Saskatoon.)

True evangelical faith is of such a nature it cannot lie dormant,
but spreads itself out in all kinds of righteousness and fruits of love;
it dies to flesh and blood;
it destroys all lusts and forbidden desires;
it seeks, serves and fears God in its inmost soul;
it clothes the naked;
it feeds the hungry;
it comforts the sorrowful;
it shelters the destitute;
it aids and consoles the sad;
it does good to those who do it harm;
it serves those that harm it;
it prays for those who persecute it;
it teaches, admonishes and judges us with the Word of the Lord;
it seeks those who are lost;
it binds up what is wounded;
it heals the sick;
it saves what is strong (sound);
it becomes all things to all people.
The persecution, suffering and anguish that come to it
for the sake of the Lord's truth
have become a glorious joy and comfort to it.

f) Pentecostal voice

contemporary

Prayer to the Holy Spirit
(by John Sloan, Horizon College and Seminary, Saskatoon)

Oh Holy Spirit
The great *ruach*
The mighty breath
Blow through us we pray
Empower us to do your will
Anoint us to preach the good news and set captives free.

Let us be a people who hunger after your spirit.
A people who do not want to go without your spirit of power.
Let us be a people who do not depend on ourselves,
on our wisdom or our love.

Breathe on us *ruach* of God.
Make your presence known to us. In and through our lives.
May your love be poured out in our hearts
so that we may love those around us.

Oh Holy Fire
Cleanse us we pray
Burn away the things that do not bear fruit.
Grow in us the fruits of your spirit.
Kill our ego and our pride and the things that keep us separate
from you and from unity with your Holy and chosen people.

Oh Living Water
Immerse us in your love
Immerse us in your spirit
Flow through us into others
Bringing life to all we meet
Bringing life to our bones

Refresh us mighty Spirit
Fill us anew; we long for you in a dry and weary land where there is
no water.
You are our life source. Fill us we pray.

3. From the Lutheran Tradition

traditional

(Evangelical Lutheran Worship, p. 73)

The Church

Gracious Father, we pray for your holy catholic church. Fill it with all truth and peace. Where it is corrupt, purify it; where it is in error, direct it; where in anything it is amiss, reform it; where it is right, strengthen it; where it is in need, provide for it; where it is divided, reunite it; for the sake of Jesus Christ, your Son, our Lord. AMEN.

On Church unity

Most high and holy God, pour out upon us your one and unifying Spirit, and awaken in every confession of the whole church a holy hunger and thirst for unity in you, through Jesus Christ, our Saviour and Lord. AMEN.

foundational

("A Mighty Fortress is our God." Martin Luther is credited with both the text and the tune. The present English version is the work of the Inter-Lutheran Commission on Worship)

1   A mighty fortress is our God,
A sword and shield victorious;
He breaks the cruel oppressor's rod
And wins salvation glorious.
The old evil foe, sworn to work us woe,
With dread craft and might he arms himself to fight,
On earth he has no equal.

2   No strength of ours can match his might!
We would be lost, rejected.
But now a champion comes to fight,
Whom God himself elected.
Ask who this may be; Lord of hosts is he!
Jesus Christ, our Lord, God's only Son adored.
He holds the field victorious.

3   Though hordes of devils fill the land
All threatening to devour us,
We tremble not, unmoved we stand;
They cannot overpow'r us.
The world's prince may rage,
In fierce war engage.
He is doomed to fail;
God's judgment must prevail!
One little word subdues him.

4   God's Word forever shall abide,
No thanks to foes, who fear it;
For God himself fights by our side
With weapons of the Spirit.
If they take our house,
Goods, fame, child or spouse,
Wrench our life away,
They cannot win the day.
The Kingdom's ours forever!

(Bishop Telmor Sartison, in *The Voice of One: Parables from Life*)

God, maybe I'll never really understand
what "In Christ" really means
but I think it has to do with these people
who are also part of
his body.
Thank you for that and them.
…
Dear Lord,
I guess I have more questions
than I have answers.
Accept my questions
coming to you as this creature's praise.
Maybe it's the questions that make me
more dependent on you. AMEN.

4. From the Orthodox Tradition

traditional

Great Compline

(Night Prayer, Orthodox hours of prayer)

O Christ our God, who at all times and at every hour, both in
heaven and on earth,
are worshipped and glorified,
long-suffering and plenteous in mercy and compassion;
who love the just and show mercy to the sinners;
who call all men to salvation through the promise of the blessings
to come:
Do you, the same Lord, receive also our supplications at this
present time,
and direct our lives according to your commandments.
Sanctify our souls; purify our bodies; set our minds right;
clear up our thoughts, and deliver us from every sorrow, evil and
distress.
Surround us with your holy Angels
so that being guarded and guided by their presence,
we may arrive at the unity of the faith
and the knowledge of your ineffable glory,
for blessed are you unto the ages of ages. Amen

Liturgy of St. Basil

(major Eucharistic liturgy)

Again, we pray to You,
be mindful of Your holy, catholic, and apostolic Church,
which is from one end of the inhabited earth to the other.
Grant peace to her which You have obtained
with the precious blood of Your Christ…
Strengthen also this holy house to the end of the ages…
reunite those separated; bring back those in error
and unite them to Your holy, catholic, and apostolic Church . . .
Prevent schism in the Church; pacify the raging of the heathen.
Quickly stop the uprisings of heresies by the power of Your Holy
Spirit.
Receive us all into Your kingdom.
Declare us to be sons and daughters of the light and of the day.
Grant us Your peace and love, Lord our God,
for you have given all things to us.

Priest: And grant that with one voice and one heart
we may glorify and praise Your most honoured and majestic name,
of the Father and the Son and the Holy Spirit,
now and forever and to the ages of ages.

Deacon: Having prayed for the unity of the faith
and for the communion of the Holy Spirit,
let us commit ourselves, and one another, and our whole life to
Christ our God.

5. From the Presbyterian Churches

traditional

For Other Churches
(Book of Common Worship, Presbyterian Church (USA) 1994, 719)

Almighty God, in Jesus Christ you called disciples and prayed for them to be joined in faith. We pray for Christian churches from which we are separated. Let us never be so sure of ourselves that we condemn the faith of others or refuse reunion with them, but make us ever ready to reach out for more truth, so that your church may be one in the Spirit; through Jesus Christ our Lord. AMEN.

traditional

For Church unity
(Book of Common Worship, Presbyterian Church (USA) 1994, 717)

Holy God, giver of peace, author of truth, we confess that we are divided and at odds with one another, that a bad spirit has arisen among us and set us against your Holy Spirit of peace and love. Take from us the mistrust, partisan spirit, contention, and all evil that now divides us. Work in us a desire for reconciliation, so that, putting aside personal grievances, we may go about your business with a single mind, devoted to our Lord and Saviour, Jesus Christ. AMEN.

A prayer of thanks for One Baptism

(Reverend Amanda Currie, Saskatoon)

God of grace and love,
today I remember my baptism, and I give thanks to you.
I give you thanks because my baptism assures me that I belong to
you.
In life and death, my greatest comfort
is that I belong to my faithful Saviour Jesus Christ.

I remember that I was baptized by a particular church,
and I give thanks for the gifts of that church,
for its faithfulness, its love,
and its commitment to walk with me on my journey
and to nurture me in faith and discipleship.

I remember that I was baptized into the one, holy, catholic church,
and I give thanks that I truly belong to that one church.
Baptism is a sign and seal of our union with Christ
and with his church — the One Church, the Body of Christ,
the Family of God, the Vine into which we are engrafted.

Gracious God,
help me to remember my baptism each day,
and to remember that as I am connected to Christ,
I am connected to all Christians.
By the gift of your Holy Spirit
help me to grow in faith, in service, in discipleship,
and in unity with my sisters and brothers in Christ.

May those who are united in baptism
soon experience that unity at the Lord's Table. AMEN.

6. From the Roman Catholic Church

foundational

(St. Cyprian, *On the Lord's Prayer*, 23: CSEL 3, 284-285)

The prayer of every Christian:
"God does not accept the sacrifice of a sower of disunion, but commands that he depart from the altar so that he may first be reconciled with his brother. For God can be appeased only by prayers that make peace. To God, the better offering is peace, brotherly concord, and a people made one in the unity of the Father, Son, and Holy Spirit."

liturgical

(from the *Roman Missal* 2011, Mass for the unity of Christians, Collect 2, p. 1264)

Attend with favour to the prayers of your people,
we ask, O Lord,
and grant that the hearts of believers
may be reunited in your praise and in repentance together,
so that, with division among Christians overcome,
we may hasten with joy to your eternal Kingdom
in the perfect communion of the Church.

Through our Lord Jesus Christ, your Son,
who lives and reigns with you in the unity of the Holy Spirit,
one God, for ever and ever. AMEN.

(Fr. Paul Couturier, pioneer in ecumenism, France, 1940s and 1950s; translated
from the French by Fr. Bernard de Margerie)

Lord Jesus, on the night before you died for us,
you prayed that all your disciples would be perfectly one,
as you are in the Father and your Father is in you.
Make us feel to the point of sorrow
the unfaithfulness of our dis-unity.
Grant us the loyalty to recognize,
and the courage to reject, the mutual indifference,
mistrust and even hostility hiding within ourselves.
Grant us to meet in you
so that from our souls and lips may ascend without cease,
the prayer for the unity of Christians, as you will it, by the means
that you will. In you, who are perfect Charity, grant us to find the
way that leads to unity, in obedience to your love and your truth.
AMEN.

(Bishop Donald Bolen, Saskatoon)

Lord God, you have revealed yourself to us as
a communion of persons, Father, Son and Holy Spirit,
yet fully one.
And you have made us in your own image and likeness,
planting deep within us a desire for unity,
for communion with you and with all those who bear your image.
Help us to be faithful to that desire for unity.
Make us artisans of reconciliation amidst the divisions of your church.
Guide us as we learn to share our lives together,
receiving gifts of the Spirit from each other,
and jointly participating in your healing mission
amidst the fragmentation and brokenness of your world.
Together may we joyfully and courageously give witness
to your saving presence in our history, in our world and in our lives.
Stir within us the desire to gather often in prayer,
rejoicing in your saving work,
giving thanks for your bounteous blessings,
bringing before you the needs of our communities and our world,
and holding fast to your own prayer that we be one,
that we might be who you created us to be,
and that the world may believe.
To you, Father, Son and Holy Spirit, source of all unity,
be glory and honour forever and ever. AMEN.

7. From the United Church of Canada

traditional

(Service Book, 1969: For the Church)

O almighty God, who hast built thy church upon the foundation of the apostles and prophets, Jesus Christ himself being the head corner stone: grant us so to be joined together in unity of spirit by their doctrine, that we may be made a holy temple acceptable unto thee; through Jesus Christ our Lord. AMEN.

contemporary

(*Celebrate God's Presence*: A Book of Service, 2000 by Ted Dodd)

O God, none of us are the same.
We have different gifts and abilities.
> **Yet, you love each of us**
> **And long for us to love one another.**
You, O Christ, prayed, "that all might be one."
> **Yet, we are divided and separated from one another.**
You, O Spirit, call us to be one body.
> **Yet, we are fractured and splintered as a church.**
O God, in your love, unite us.
> **O Christ, make us one in love.**
O Spirit, may the whole world know our faith
through our loving action.
> **AMEN.**

(Rev. Ron McConnell, Saskatoon)

God, you call us to be the church of Jesus Christ.
Increase our love for one another, we pray.
Inspire our worship, work and witness to better reflect your grace.
As Jesus crossed boundaries of separation and division to heal and reconcile,
empower us to cross such boundaries in our day:

to breach walls of rigidity and self-righteousness within and around the church;

to bridge chasms created by poverty and wealth, racism and sexism, and by fear.

Help us to receive the gifts of your Spirit revealed in others,

in their cultures and traditions, liturgical practices and theological insights.

As your church, the Body of Christ in the world, help us to be

a justice-seeking, peace-making, healing and reconciling people of faith,

as followers of Jesus, the Sun of Righteousness, the Prince of Peace,

our Healer and our Reconciliation. AMEN.

Universal Prayers

From the World Council of Churches and the Pontifical Council for
the Promotion of Christian Unity (Roman Catholic)

1. Prayer for Christian unity

(from the WCC, Fifth World Conference on Faith & Order, 1993)

O God, holy and eternal Trinity,
we pray for your church in the world.
Sanctify its life; renew its worship;
empower its witness; heal its divisions;
make visible its unity.

Lead us, with all our brothers and sisters,
towards communion in faith, life and witness so that,
united in one body by the one Spirit,
we may together witness to the perfect unity of your love.
AMEN.

2. Prayer for the churches

(from the Week of Prayer, 2000)

O God, you have established your presence
among us
in the body of Christ, your church:
praise and glory be to you!
Help us to follow your will,
that those who belong to you may be one.
Open our eyes to accept one another
as brothers and sisters
so that we may open our arms
to embrace those who are different.

Help us to see the work of your Spirit
in other churches,
and urge us to work together towards unity
so that the world may believe,
to the praise of your glory.
AMEN.

3. Prayer for the world

(from the Week of Prayer, 2000)

O God, under your wing
you gather the whole of creation:
praise and glory to you!
Help us to follow your will,
to gather up all things in Christ.
Open our eyes to see the riches of your grace,
so that we may open our mouths to proclaim
the hope for the world which lies in you.
Help us to work for a world
where people of different religions and cultures
can live together in peace;
for a just world where rich and poor
share their resources.
Help us to use the gifts of your creation
according to your wisdom,
to the praise of your glory.
AMEN.

4. The way of the cross
(from the Week of Prayer, 2001)

Leader: Let us look to Jesus, the pioneer and perfecter of our faith.
All: Jesus Christ, we look upon your cross.
Standing before it, we come to you.
Your cross shows us the way.
Because your sacrifice was for all of us,
your cross points the way from separation to unity.
Because you defeated death forever,
your cross opens the way from death to life.
Your resurrection calls us to a joy
that no one can take from us.

L: Jesus Christ, you are the resurrection and the life. We worship you.
All: AMEN

5. Seeking the unity of one family
(from the Week of Prayer, 2002)

Creator of us all,
you put into our hearts
the longing for community with you.
Fulfill those desires, we pray.
Reunite us into one family through Jesus Christ,
who lives and reigns in communion
with you and the Holy Spirit. AMEN.

6. Intercession
(from the Week of Prayer, 2002)

We pray for the people of our world
so often torn by war or suffering from disaster.
We pray also for all in our own country
who experience abuse at the hands of others,
who are homeless or in deep poverty,
who despair of any change in their lives.
We also pray for all who would bring light
into the darkened corners of our world.
May they be your healing messengers to the world.
May we also be challenged to such ministry,
where we live, as followers of Christ.
AMEN.

7. Asking for the grace of healed unity
(from the Week of Prayer, 2012)

Loving and merciful God,
teach us the joy of sharing in Your peace.
Fill us with Your Holy Spirit so that we may tear down
the walls of hostility separating us.
May the risen Christ, who is our peace,
help us to overcome all division
and unite us as members of His household.
We ask this in the name of Jesus Christ,
to whom with You and the Holy Spirit,
be all honour and glory, world without end.
AMEN.

8. Confession and forgiveness

(from the Week of Prayer, 2013)

In humility we come to your feet, dear God,
as we remember our sinfulness and the disunity
for which we have been responsible.
We confess that we preserve the inherited human barriers
of caste, class, ethnicity, power
and all things that keep Christians apart.
We ask for your forgiveness
that we have often used our history and our past
as churches to discriminate against one another
and hurt the unity to which Christ has called us.
Forgive us our disunity
and help us to continue to strive for unity,
in the precious name of Jesus your Son.
AMEN.

9. Prayer for the churches

(from the WCC, 10th Assembly, November 2013)

O God of life,
lead us to justice and peace,
that suffering people may discover hope;
the scarred world find healing;
and the divided churches become visibly one,
through the one who prayed for us,
and in whom we are one Body,
your Son, Jesus Christ,
who with you and the Holy Spirit,
is worthy to be praised, one God,
now and forever.
AMEN.

10. Commitment to unity

(from Week of Prayer, 2014)

Leader: Paul challenged the Christians in Corinth to know in their hearts and to show in their actions that Christ has not been divided. He challenges us, too, to realize more fully that unity we already have in Christ. With all those in every place who call on the Lord Jesus Christ,
Congregation: Together, we are called to be saints.

L: Graced by God in every way,
C: Together, we give thanks for one another.

L: Rich in the many blessings God has given us through our union in Christ,
C: Together, we are not lacking in any spiritual gifts.

L: Sure in the God who strengthens us for love and service,
C: Together, we affirm that God is faithful.

L: Embraced by Jesus Christ,
C: Together, we are called into fellowship.

L: United in the same mind and the same purpose,
C: Together, we seek to be in agreement.

L: Overcoming our quarrels about the one who was crucified for us,
C: Together, we belong to Christ.

L: Has Christ, then, been divided?
C: No! Together, we go into the world to proclaim his good news!

PART FOUR

RESOURCE TEXTS: FOOD FOR DISCERNMENT

"That you may be filled
with the knowledge of God's will
in all spiritual wisdom
and understanding."

Colossians 1: 9b

INTRODUCTION

PART FOUR OFFERS A SERIES OF SHORT EXCERPTS from a few of the best ecumenical sources available at this time in the life of the Church. They are intended to foster reflection, leading to a new discernment, on the part of churches and individual Christians, of the call of Christ to the unity of his Body and the efforts of churches today to respond to that call.

Come, Holy Spirit! Visit the hearts of the faithful. Kindle in them the fire of your love. AMEN.

1. Unto the churches of Christ everywhere

Encyclical Letter of the Ecumenical Patriarchate (1920)

Love one another from the heart (1 Peter 1: 22).

Our own church holds that rapprochement between the various Christian churches and fellowship between them is not excluded by the doctrinal differences which exist between them. In our opinion such a rapprochement is highly desirable and necessary. It would be useful in many ways for the real interest of each particular church and of the whole Christian body, and also for the preparation and advancement of that blessed union

which will be completed in the future in accordance with the will of God. We therefore consider that the present time is most favourable for bringing forward this important question and studying it together.

This pioneering text was written in 1920. How has there been "rapprochement" between the various Christian churches in the past century?

2. "We intend to stay together"

World Council of Churches, First Assembly, Amsterdam (1948)

We are divided from one another not only in matters of faith, order and tradition, but also by pride of nation, class and race. But Christ has made us His own, and He is not divided. In seeking Him, we find one another. Here at Amsterdam, we have committed ourselves afresh to Him, and have covenanted with one another in constituting this World Council of Churches. We intend to stay together. We call upon Christian congregations everywhere to endorse and fulfill this covenant in their relations with one another. In thankfulness to God, we commit the future to Him.

Today, is our commitment to each other, across denominational lines, as strong?

3. Common declaration of Pope Paul VI and Patriarch Athenagoras I

December 7, 1965

"Pope Paul VI and Patriarch Athenagoras I with his synod, certain that they are expressing the common desire for justice and the unanimous sentiment of charity on the part of their faithful, and remembering the command of the Lord: "If you are offering your gift at the altar, and there remember that your brother has something against you, leave your gift before the altar and go first to be reconciled to your brother" (Matthew 5:23-24), declare with one accord that:

(a) They regret the offensive words, the reproaches without foundation and the reprehensible gestures which on both sides marked or accompanied the sad events of that period;[*]

(b) They also regret and wish to erase from the memory and midst of the Church the sentences of excommunication which followed them, and whose memory has acted as an obstacle to a rapprochement in charity down to our own age, and to consign them to oblivion.

. . .

This reciprocal act of justice and forgiveness, as Pope Paul VI and Patriarch Athenagoras I with his synod are aware, cannot suffice to put an end to the differences, ancient or more recent, which remain between the Roman Catholic Church and the Orthodox Church and which, by the action of the Holy Spirit, will be overcome, thanks to the purification of hearts, regret for historical errors, and an effective determination to arrive at a common understanding and expression of the apostolic faith and its demands.

This solemn commitment dates from 50 years ago. What are our hopes today?

---

[*] i.e., 11th century and earlier, deteriorating relations, mutual excommunications.

4. Restoration of unity

Vatican II, *Decree on Ecumenism* (November 21, 1964), introduction

The restoration of unity among all Christians is one of the principal concerns of the Second Vatican Council. . . . Certainly, such division openly contradicts the will of Christ, scandalizes the world, and damages that most holy cause, the preaching of the Gospel to every creature.

The Lord of Ages nevertheless wisely and patiently follows out the plan of His grace on our behalf, sinners that we are. In recent times, he has begun to bestow more generously upon divided Christians remorse over their divisions and longing for unity.

What have we done with the grace offered — grace of "remorse," of "longing"?

5. Gifts beyond boundaries

Vatican II, *Decree on Ecumenism* (November 21, 1964), n. 3b

Moreover, some, even very many of the most significant elements and endowments, which together go to build up and give life to the Church itself, can exist outside the visible boundaries of the Catholic Church: the written Word of God; the life of grace; faith, hope and charity, with the other interior gifts of the Holy Spirit, as well as visible elements. All of these, which come from Christ and lead back to Him, belong by right to the one Church of Christ.

Are we aware, and grateful?

6. Unity requires conversion

Vatican II, *Decree on Ecumenism* (November 21, 1964), n. 7a

There can be no ecumenism worthy of the name without interior conversion. For it is from newness of attitudes of mind (Cf. Ephesians 4: 23), from self-denial and unstinted love, that desires for unity take their rise and develop in a mature way. We should therefore pray to the Holy Spirit for the grace to be genuinely self-denying, humble, gentle in the service of others and to have an attitude of brotherly generosity toward them.

Do churches, as churches, also need the conversion spoken of here?

7. Sin and forgiveness

Vatican II, *Decree on Ecumenism* (November 21, 1964), n. 7a

St. John has testified: *"If we say we have not sinned, we make him a liar, and his Word is not in us."* (1 Jn. 1: 10). This holds good for sins against unity. Thus in humble prayer, we beg pardon of God and of our separated brethren, just as we forgive them that trespass against us.

Where is the Holy Spirit leading you, in this text?

8. Our hope is in the Trinity

Vatican II, *Decree on Ecumenism* (November 21, 1964), n. 24b

Further, this Council declares that it realizes that this holy objective
— the reconciliation of all Christians in the unity of the one and
only Church of Christ — transcends human powers and gifts. It
therefore places its hope entirely in the prayer of Christ for the
Church, in the love of the Father for us, and in the power of the
Holy Spirit: "And hope does not disappoint, because God's love has
been poured forth in our hearts through the Holy Spirit who has
been given us" (Romans 5: 5).

How strong, or fragile, is our hope regarding the healing of
divisions in the Body of Christ?

9. A discipline internal to the life of faith

In One Body Through the Cross, The Princeton Proposal for Christian Unity
(2003), n. 5b

Therefore the quest for a deeper unity among Christians is a
discipline internal to the life of faith. It has two fundamental
assumptions: (a) that Christian unity is an intrinsic part of the
transformed life God works among those who live in the faith of
Jesus, and (b) that it is a goal yet to be fully achieved in concrete,
visible human terms.

How can I articulate in simple words the discipline described
above?

10. Division, not normal

In One Body Through the Cross, The Princeton Proposal for Christian Unity
(2003), n. 10b

For where division is regarded as normal, is no longer perceived as scandal and wound, the gift of unity that is the "mystery of God's will," his "plan for the fullness of time" (Ephesians 1: 9-19) will remain hidden by human ignorance and sin. To work towards the real and concrete growth of unity among all our churches is, we believe, an imperative for the conscience of every Christian.

What may the Holy Spirit be declaring to us here?

11. Unity, a constituent goal

In One Body Through the Cross, The Princeton Proposal for Christian Unity
(2003), n. 19

A common life, in which those who were divided are reconciled in the body of Christ, is an essential goal of the mission that God has appointed for his people. Unity is not only a means to mission, but rather a constituent goal: God gathers his people precisely in order to bring unity to a divided humanity. If we accept division from other Christians as normal and inevitable, we turn away from the mission God has given us.

What would be the benefits of Christians rediscovering and implementing a common life?

12. Our differences must be questioned

In One Body Through the Cross, The Princeton Proposal for Christian Unity
(2003), n. 23

The apostolic message does not affirm diversity for its own
sake. It calls men and women of every human origin into a
holy community and confers on them a new shared identity in
confession of the crucified and risen Lord. The life of the church
thus calls for continuous critical sifting and reconstruction of
human identity. Elements that constitute our differences must be
questioned, judged, reconciled, and reconfigured within the unity
of the body of Christ.

*How are we to deal, faithfully, with "differences" among the
churches?*

13. Friendly division is still division

In One Body Through the Cross, The Princeton Proposal for Christian Unity
(2003), n. 44

But friendly division is still division. We must not let our present
division be seen as normal, as the natural expression of a Christian
marketplace with churches representing different options for a
variety of spiritual tastes. Consumerist values and an ideology of
diversity can anesthetize us to the wound of division. Recovering
from this ecumenical anesthesia is one of the strongest present
challenges to faithfulness.

*Shall we need more wisdom and courage to look at and deal
with our divisions? What shall we ask the Holy Spirit?*

14. Unity to be unambiguously visible

In One Body Through the Cross, The Princeton Proposal for Christian Unity
(2003), n. 45

We agree, however, that the unity we seek must be unambiguously
visible, "so that the world may believe" (John 17: 21). Unity must be
recognizable as unity without an extensive theological gloss. One
must be able to see that the church, in its ordinary life and practice,
is one community reconciled in Christ.

Shall we rejoice in hope?

15. A living communion, our responsibility

Pope John Paul II, *Ut Unum Sint* (1995), n. 6

The unity of all divided humanity is the will of God. For this reason
he sent his Son, so that by dying and rising for us he might bestow
on us the Spirit of love. On the eve of his sacrifice on the Cross,
Jesus himself prayed to the Father for his disciples and for all those
who believe in him, that they *might be one*, a living communion.
This is the basis not only of the duty, but also of the responsibility
before God and his plan, which falls to those who through Baptism
become members of the Body of Christ, a Body in which the
fullness of reconciliation and communion must be made present.

*What is the responsibility we bear, as a consequence of our
belonging to the Body of Christ?*

16. Prayer draws us to unity

Pope John Paul II, *Ut Unum Sint* (1995), n. 22a

When Christians pray together, the goal of unity seems closer. The long history of Christians marked by many divisions seems to converge once more because it tends towards the Source of its unity which is Jesus Christ. He "is the same yesterday, today and forever!" (Hebrews 13: 8). In the fellowship of prayer Christ is truly present; he prays "in us," "with us," and "for us."

Do you/we ever pray meaningfully for the healing of divisions and the fuller unity of the churches?

17. Purification through dialogue

Pope John Paul II, *Ut Unum Sint* (1995), n. 28b-29

Dialogue is not simply an exchange of ideas. In some way it is always an "exchange of gifts."

29. For this reason, the Council's Decree on Ecumenism also emphasizes the importance of "every effort to eliminate words, judgments, and actions which do not respond to the condition of separated brethren with truth and fairness and so make mutual relations between them more difficult."

How do we think, and talk, about members of other churches — as true sisters and brothers in Christ —?

18. Love for the truth

Pope John Paul II, *Ut Unum Sint* (1995), n. 36b

Love for the truth is the deepest dimension of any authentic quest for full communion between Christians. Without this love it would be impossible to face the objective theological, cultural, psychological and social difficulties which appear when disagreements are examined. This dimension, which is interior and personal, must be inseparably accompanied by a spirit of charity and humility.

Love for the truth . . . a spirit of charity and humility — straight out of Saint Paul's teachings!

19. Helping each other toward fullness

Pope John Paul II, *Ut Unum Sint* (1995), n. 78b

Ecumenism implies that the Christian communities should help one another so that there may be truly present in them the full content and all the requirements of "the heritage handed down by the Apostles" (Decree on Ecumenism, n. 14). Without this, full communion will never be possible. This mutual help in the search of truth is a sublime form of evangelical charity.

How much further must we travel until this "mutual help in the search of truth" becomes a true passion at the heart of the churches?

20. Conversion to fellowship
Pope John Paul II, *Ut Unum Sint* (1995), n. 84e

Where there is a sincere desire to follow Christ, the Spirit is often able to pour out his grace in extraordinary ways. The experience of ecumenism has enabled us to understand this better. If, in the interior spiritual space described above, Communities are able truly to "be converted" to the quest for full and visible communion, God will do for them what he did for their Saints. He will overcome the obstacles inherited from the past and will lead Communities along his paths to where he wills: to the visible *koinonia* which is both praise of his glory and service of his plan of salvation.

Do we dare let our faith and hope soar to such heights of faithfulness?

21. Baptism, eucharist, ministry
WCC, Faith and Order Commission, *Baptism, Eucharist and Ministry* (1982), Preface, p. viii

If the divided churches are to achieve the visible unity they seek, one of the essential prerequisites is that they should be in basic agreement on baptism, eucharist and ministry.

How do I react to this statement, and why?

22. Working at doctrinal convergences

WCC, Faith and Order Commission, *Baptism, Eucharist and Ministry* (1982),

Preface, p. ix

In the process of growing together in mutual trust, the churches must develop these doctrinal convergences step by step, until they are finally able to declare together that they are living in communion with one another in continuity with the apostles and the teachings of the universal church.

Am I encouraging my church to join and persevere in this "process of growing together in mutual trust" with other churches?

23. Mutual recognition of baptism

WCC, Faith and Order Commission, *Baptism, Eucharist and Ministry* (1982),

Baptism 15

Mutual recognition of baptism is acknowledged as an important sign and means of expressing the baptismal unity given in Christ. Wherever possible, mutual recognition should be expressed explicitly by the churches.

Are the churches making progress in this regard?

24. "Christ gathers, teaches, and nourishes the Church"
WCC, Faith and Order Commission, *Baptism, Eucharist and Ministry* (1982)

Eucharist, 1b

It (the eucharist) has acquired many names: for example, the Lord's Supper, the breaking of bread, the holy communion, the divine liturgy, the mass. Its celebration continues as the central act of the Church's worship (n. 29). In the celebration of the eucharist, Christ gathers, teaches and nourishes the Church. It is Christ who invites to the meal and who presides at it. He is the shepherd who leads the people of God, the prophet who announces the Word of God, the priest who celebrates the mystery of God. In most churches, this presidency is signified by an ordained minister.

What are your thoughts, what might your prayer be, regarding this statement?

25. How is the life of the Church to be ordered?
WCC, Faith and Order Commission, *Baptism, Eucharist and Ministry* (1982)

Ministry, 6

Though the churches are agreed in their general understanding of the calling of the people of God, they differ in their understanding of how the life of the Church is to be ordered. In particular, there are differences concerning the place and forms of the ordained ministry. As they engage in the effort to overcome these differences, the churches need to work from the perspective of the calling of the whole people of God. A common answer needs to be found to the following question: How, according to the will of God and under the guidance of the Holy Spirit, is the life of the Church to be understood and ordered, so that the Gospel may be spread and the community built up in love?

What are your thoughts about this statement?

26. By grace alone . . . justified

Lutheran-Roman Catholic International Commission, *Joint Declaration on the Doctrine of Justificatrion* (1999). n. 15

In faith we together hold the conviction that justification is the work of the triune God. The Father sent his Son into the world to save sinners. The foundation and presupposition of justification is the incarnation, death and resurrection of Christ. Justification thus means that Christ himself is our righteousness, in which we share through the Holy Spirit in accord with the will of the Father. Together we confess: By grace alone, in faith in Christ's saving work and not because of any merit on our part, we are accepted by God and receive the Holy Spirit, who renews our hearts while equipping and calling us to good works.

What prayer impulse does the above statement evoke in you?

27. May the Holy Spirit lead us further . . .

Lutheran-Roman Catholic International Commission, *Joint Declaration on the Doctrine of Justificatrion* (1999). n. 43-44

n. 43 Our consensus in basic truths of the doctrine of justification must come to influence the life and teachings of our churches. Here it must prove itself. . . . The Lutheran churches and the Roman Catholic Church will continue to strive together to deepen this common understanding of justification and to make it bear fruit in the life and teaching of the churches.

n. 44 We give thanks to the Lord for this decisive step forward on the way to overcoming the division of the churches. We ask the Holy Spirit to lead us further towards that visible unity which is Christ's will?

Can you discern any concrete way(s) the above undertaking might begin to take shape in the churches?

28. Preparing for the 500th anniversary . . .

Lutheran-Roman Catholic International Commission, *From Conflict to Communion* (2013), Introduction

n. 1 In 2017, Lutheran and Catholic Christians will commemorate together the 500th anniversary of the beginning of the Reformation. Lutherans and Catholics today enjoy a growth in mutual understanding, cooperation, and respect. They have come to acknowledge that more unites than divides them: above all, common faith in the Triune God and the revelation in Jesus Christ, as well as recognition of the basic truth of the doctrine of justification. . . .

n. 3 The upcoming year of 2017 challenges Catholics and Lutherans to discuss in dialogue the issues and consequences of the Wittenberg Reformation, which centered on the person and thought of Martin Luther, and to develop perspectives for the remembrance and appropriation of the Reformation today. Luther's reforming agenda poses a spiritual and theological challenge to both contemporary Catholics and Lutherans.

Doesn't this Introduction lead us to new thoughts, and open up new possibilities, for Lutherans and Catholics (and other Christians) to draw closer together in Christ Jesus?

29. "Partnership in mission"

International Anglican-Roman Catholic Commission for Unity and Mission,
Growing Together in Unity and Mission (2007), n. 7.10

It must be acknowledged that the progress towards agreement
in faith achieved through the theological dialogue has been
substantial, but that in the past four decades we have only just
begun to give tangible expression to the incontrovertible elements
of shared faith. Even in a time of uncertainty, the mission given us
by Christ obliges and compels us to seek to engage more deeply and
widely in a partnership in mission, coupled with common witness
and joint prayer.

While this may not be the moment to initiate a formal new stage
in our relations, we believe that it is the time to bridge the gap
between the elements of faith we hold in common and the tangible
expression of that shared belief in our ecclesial lives.

*How can we give "tangible expression," in the life of the Church,
to those things we believe in common?*

30. "The gifts we truly have to offer"

International Methodist-Roman Catholic Dialogue, *The Grace Given to You in Christ* (2006), n. 97

The very considerable agreement reached over the years of our recent dialogue . . . indicates that Catholics and Methodists do, in fact, hold in common many beliefs and priorities regarding the Church. It is time now to return to the concrete reality of one another, to look one another in the eye, and with love and esteem to acknowledge what we see to be truly of Christ and of the Gospel, and thereby of the Church, in one another. Doing so will highlight the way for an exchange of gifts which is what ecumenical dialogue, in some way, always is (Ut Unum Sint, n. 28). In our striving for full communion, "we dare not lose any of the gifts with which the Holy Spirit has endowed our communities in their separation." The Holy Spirit is the true giver of the gifts we are seeking to exchange.

What spiritual gifts do you think your church has to offer, and what gifts are you willing to receive from other churches?

31. Convergence: humble, obedient steps . . .

WCC, Faith and Order Commission, *The Church: Towards a Common Vision*
(2013) Preface

The convergence reached in *The Church* represents an
extraordinary ecumenical achievement. . . . In the long process
from 1993-2012, the theological expressions and ecclesial
experiences of many churches have been brought together in such
a way that the churches reading this text may find themselves
challenged to live more fully the ecclesial life; others may find
in it aspects of ecclesial life and understanding which have been
neglected or forgotten; others may find themselves strengthened
and affirmed. As Christians experience life-long growth into Christ,
they will find themselves growing closer to one another,
and living into the biblical image of the one body: "For in the one
Spirit we were all baptized into one body — Jews or Greeks, slaves
or free — and we were all made to drink of the one Spirit."

*What an extraordinary reflection! What an invitation to the
churches!*

32. Christ's will for and gift of unity

WCC, Faith and Order Commission, *The Church: Towards a Common Vision*

(2013) n. 1

"Thy will be done" are words that countless believers from all Christian churches pray every day. Jesus himself prayed similar words in the garden of Gethsemane shortly before his arrest (cf. Mt. 26:39-42; Mark 14:36; Luke 22:42). In John's gospel, moreover, he revealed his will for the Church when he prayed to the Father that all of his disciples be one, so that the world may believe (cf. John 17:21). To pray that the Lord's will be done thus necessarily requires a wholehearted endeavour to embrace his will for and gift of unity. The present text — *The Church: Towards a Common Vision* — addresses what many consider to be the most difficult issues facing the churches in overcoming any remaining obstacles to their living out the Lord's gift of communion: our understanding of the nature of the Church itself. The great importance of that gift and goal highlights the significance of the issues to be treated in the pages that follow.

How marvellous that theologians of (almost) all churches can speak in such a biblically inspired way, serenely yet fervently, about Christ's costly gift of unity — already here, yet lying ahead of us? Let's re-read from the heart.

33. "God's work of healing"

WCC, Faith and Order Commission, *The Church: Towards a Common Vision* (2013) n. 1

The Church, as the body of Christ, acts by the power of the Holy Spirit to continue his life-giving mission in prophetic and compassionate ministry and so participate in God's work of healing a broken world. Communion, whose source is the very life of the Holy Trinity, is both the gift by which the Church lives and, at the same time, the gift that God calls the Church to offer to a wounded and divided humanity in hope of reconciliation and healing.

Can we already here begin to sense the deep God-driven being and mission of Christ's Church?

34. The Church, called and sent

WCC, Faith and Order Commission, *The Church: Towards a Common Vision* (2013) n. 13

As a divinely established communion, the Church belongs to God and does not exist for itself. It is by its very nature missionary, called and sent to witness in its own life to that communion which God intends for all humanity and for all creation in the kingdom.

*How best can the Church manifest **in its own life** that "communion" which God intends for the whole universe?*

35. Elements required for full communion

WCC, Faith and Order Commission, *The Church: Towards a Common Vision* (2013) n. 37

The journey towards the full realization of God's gift of communion requires Christian communities to agree about the fundamental aspects of the life of the Church. "The ecclesial elements required for full communion within a visibly united church — the goal of the ecumenical movement — are communion in the fullness of apostolic faith; in sacramental life; in a truly one and mutually recognized ministry; in structures of conciliar relations and decision-making; and in common witness and service in the world." ("The Church: Local and Universal," n. 25). These attributes serve as a necessary framework for maintaining unity in legitimate diversity.

How do you consider and assess the requirements listed above for a denomination to be "truly and fully church"?

36. Unity in the Church

Third Lausanne Congress on World Evangelization, *The Cape Town Commitment* (2010), p. 65-66

A divided Church has no message for a divided world. Our failure to live in reconciled unity is a major obstacle to authenticity and effectiveness in mission. We lament the dividedness and divisiveness of our churches and organizations. We deeply and urgently long for Christians to cultivate a spirit of grace and to be obedient to Paul's command to 'make every effort to maintain the unity of the Spirit in the bond of peace.' While we recognize that our deepest unity is spiritual, we long for greater recognition of the missionary power of visible, practical, earthly unity. So we urge Christian sisters and brothers worldwide, for the sake of our common witness and mission, to resist the temptation to split the body of Christ, and to seek the paths of reconciliation and restored unity wherever possible.

What expressions, or groups of words, strike you the most in this quotation – and why?

37. Our commitment — part 1

WCC, 10th Assembly, *Unity Statement* (2013), n. 15

In faithfulness to this our common calling, we will seek together the full visible unity of the One, Holy, Catholic and Apostolic Church when we shall express our unity around the one Table of the Lord. In pursuing the unity of the Church we will open ourselves to receive the gifts of each other's tradition, and offer our gifts to one another. We will learn to commemorate together the martyrs who witnessed to our common faith. We will continue theological conversations, giving attention to new voices and different methods of approach. We will seek to live out the consequences of our theological agreements.

What are the six commitments made here by the World Council?

38. Our commitment — part 2

WCC, 10th Assembly, *Unity Statement* (2013), n. 15

We will intensify our work for justice, peace and the healing of creation, and address together the complex challenges of contemporary social, economic and moral issues. We will work for more just, participatory and inclusive ways of living together. We will make common cause for the well-being of humanity and creation with those of other faith communities. We will hold each other accountable for fulfilling these commitments. Above all, we will pray without ceasing for the unity for which Jesus prayed (John 17): a unity of faith, love and compassion that Jesus Christ brought through his ministry; a unity like the unity Christ shares with the Father; a unity enfolded in the communion of the life and love of the Triune God. Here, we receive the mandate for the Church's vocation for unity in mission and service.

What further commitments are listed here?

39. "Pilgrims journeying alongside one another"

Pope Francis, *Evangelii Gaudium* (2013), nn. 244-246

Commitment to ecumenism responds to the prayer of the Lord Jesus that "they may all be one" (John 17:21) . . . We must never forget that we are pilgrims journeying together alongside one another. This means that we must have sincere trust in our fellow pilgrims, putting aside all suspicion and distrust, and turn our gaze to what we are all seeking: the radiant face of God's peace. Trusting others is an art and peace is an art. Jesus told us: "Blessed are the peacemakers" (Matthew 5:9) In taking up this task, also among ourselves, we fulfill the ancient prophecy: "They shall beat their swords into ploughshares" (Isaiah 2:4).

. . .

If we really believe in the abundantly free-working of the Holy Spirit, we can learn so much from one another! It is not just about being better informed about others, but rather about reaping what the Spirit has sown in them, which is also meant to be a gift for us.

How can trust grow between Christians of different denominations, according to the will of Christ?

GATHERED TOGETHER:
Ecumenical Prayer Services for Christian Reconciliation and Unity

"There can be
no ecumenism
worthy of the name
without a change of heart."

Vatican II, Decree on Ecumenism, n. 7

INTRODUCTION

"There can be no ecumenism worthy of the name without
a change of heart. . . . This change of heart and holiness
of life, along with public and private prayer for the unity
of Christians, should be regarded as the soul of the whole
ecumenical movement, and can rightly be called 'spiritual
ecumenism.'"

(Vatican II, *Decree on Ecumenism,* nn. 7 and 8)

AT THE HEART OF SPIRITUAL ECUMENISM is prayer, and prayer in
common. Hence, Part Five offers a series of Ecumenical Prayer
Services/Liturgies entitled *Gathered Together* — an effort to
promote interdenominational *community* prayer, especially at the
local level (local congregations/parishes, Christian associations
or small group meetings, etc.). They may also be of service in the
prayer life of larger gatherings.

One deliberate feature of these texts is the use, explicit
or implicit, of ecumenical documents published by formal
international dialogue groups, over the last 45 or so years. Themes
drawn from such documents provide much of the theological
orientation and content of the prayer services.

I sincerely hope that efforts of comprehension and preparation
leading to the celebration in common of these *Gathered Together*
services will be blessed and fruitful, in the power of the Holy Spirit,
for the sake of the body of Christ, the Church, in fulfillment of the
Father's merciful plan of salvation for all humankind.

A measure of flexibility and creativity, depending on local or
other circumstances, is certainly commendable –along with the
hope that the overall orientation, theme and format of each Service
will be honoured.

PRACTICAL SUGGESTIONS

1. It is highly recommended to assign the various ministries involved in these Ecumenical Prayer Services among women and men, youth, etc.

2. The celebration of these Services cannot and ought not to be improvised. Due preparation and some rehearsal(s), as warranted, will prove to be most beneficial. As a rule, it would seem appropriate to aim for a 30-40 minutes length for each service.

3. Attention to singing and other music: it was not within the competence of the author of this book to indicate or suggest particular hymns, chants, refrains, acclamations, instrumental features, etc. to be used for and within each Prayer Service. One cannot underestimate, however, the pastoral and esthetical importance of this feature. In this regard, a list of suitable hymns may be found on the following page. Hopefully, this will be of some help to those persons in the parish/local congregation who have accepted the responsibility of preparing the Services.

4. Note for homilists or preachers: a suggestion is made that the prayer formats offered here might include a bilateral sermon or homily. This means the latter would be delivered by two persons in dialogue, belonging to two different churches / denominations. If you are inclined to pursue this suggestion, please consult *Suggestions for homilists/preachers regarding bilateral sermons/homilies* on the next page.

SUGGESTIONS FOR HOMILISTS/PREACHERS
REGARDING BILATERAL HOMILIES

1. The purpose of bilateral homilies is to give responsible *common witness* to the Christian faith, where possible, despite remaining divisions between churches.

2. There will obviously need to be some *joint* study of the Scripture text(s), and a discussion regarding how to divide up the particular teaching/exhortation points to be made. The discussion should lead to a clear and trustful agreement of who will deal with what point, and in what order.

3. This type of preaching invites the two homilists to dovetail the teachings they wish to expound — so that the preaching does not fly off in all directions, and perhaps even express contradictory teachings. If pastorally helpful, and agreed upon, divergence(s) may be expressed soberly, in a spirit of respect, of hope, and of sharing each other's (perceived) burden.

4. Such bilateral preaching, if attempted responsibly, presumes *a strong degree of trust* between preachers and within the interdenominational congregation gathered in the Service.

5. The homiletic mode is intended more as an act of witness and encouragement to discipleship, than as one of strict teaching.

6. It is not a "show" or a stage for competition or one-upmanship!

7. Since the homily will necessarily be short (10-12 min, max.), make sure your content is limited and of realistic length.

8. The two homilists would preferably speak from two different microphones, close to each other and in comfortable view of each other.

9. In all this, may the ministry of preaching be worthy of the Gospel, and faithful to the reconciling Church.

LIST OF SUITABLE HYMNS

Hymn Book Abbreviations

BOP = The Book of Praise (Presbyterian)
CBWIII = Catholic Book of Worship III (Roman Catholic)
CP = Common Praise (Anglican)
G&P = Glory & Praise (Roman Catholic)
MV = More Voices (United)
S&S #1 = Spirit & Song #1 (Roman Catholic)
VU = Voices United (United)

Hymns for Unity

Abba, Father, G&P 696

A new commandment, BOP 225

Behold how pleasant, how good it is, CP 473, VU 856

Blest be the tie that binds, BOP 481, CP 507, VU 602

Break not the circle of enabling love, CBWIII 524

Brother, sister, let me serve you, BOP 635/We are pilgrims VU 595

By the waking of our hearts, S&S#1 102

Christ, from whom all blessings flow, CBWIII 525

Christ is made the sure foundation, BOP 482, CBWIII 430, CP 300, VU 325

Christ is the King! CBWIII 387

Come now, O God of peace, VU 34/Come now, O Prince of Peace, CP 588

Companions on the journey, G&P 566

Draw the circle wide, CP 418, MV 145

Eternal Ruler of the ceaseless round, CP 497

Filled with the Spirit's power, BOP 282, CBWIII 413, CP 658, VU 194

For all the saints, BOP 611, CBWIII 449, CP 276, G&P 445, VU 705

Forth in the peace of Christ we go, CBWIII 514

Gather us in, CBWIII 587/Here in this place new light is streaming, CP 465

Gather us together, CBWIII 601, G&P 534

Gather your people, G&P 529, S&S#1 111

Go to the world, CP 598, VU 420

God bless your church with strength, BOP 491

God is love, CBWII 473

God is love, and where true love is, BOP 227

God of all the world, MV 22

God who spread the boundless prairie, MV 53

Healer of our every ill, CP 612, VU 619

Heaven is singing for joy, VU 230

Help us to help each other, Lord, BOP 489

Here, O God, your servants gather, CP 534, VU 362

In Christ there is no east or west, BOP 480, CBWIII 529, CP 484, G&P 565, VU 606

In loving partnership we come, BOP 759, VU 603

Let all things now living, BOP 338, CP 403, VU 242

Let us build a house (All are welcome), MV 1

Like the murmur of the dove's song, BOP 385, CP 635, VU 205

Many are the light beams, VU 588

O for a world where everyone, BOP 730/Let there be light, VU 679

O laughing light, BOP 823, CP 18, VU 434

One Lord, G&P 453

One Spirit, One Church, G&P 570, S&S#1 132

Sing a new Church, G&P 572

Sisters let us walk together, MV 179

Spirit of the living God, BOP 400, CP 647, VU 376

The church's one foundation, BOP 479, CBWIII 526, CP 525, G&P 573, VU 331

The day you gave us, BOP 826, VU 437/The day thou gavest, CP 29

The Kingdom of God, MV 146

There is One Lord, CBWIII 530

There is room for all, MV 62

Ubi caritas, CBWIII 67, G&P 364

Where true love and charity are found (Ubi cartas), CBWIII 376

We are all one people, MV 141

We are God's people, BOP 472

We are one in the Spirit, BOP 471/They'll know we are Christians, G&P 568

We praise you, O God, BOP 425, CP 342, VU 218

Where charity and love prevail, BOP 692, G&P 644, CP 487

Who is my mother? MV 178

With one voice, S&S#1 147

Your hand, O God, has guided, BOP 477, CP 444, VU 274

Eucharistic Hymns for Unity

At that first Eucharist, G&P 511

Behold the Lamb, G&P 524

Bread of life, CBWIII 597, G&P 498

Bread of life, G&P 522, S&S#1 150

Christians, let us love one another, CBWIII 595

Father, we thank thee who hast planted, CP 81

I come with joy, BOP 530, CBWIII 424, CP 60, VU 477

Jesus calls us here to meet him, BOP 528,CP 59

Lead us to your table, S&S#1 155

Let us talents and tongues employ, BOP 563, VU 468

One bread, one body, BOP 540, CP 73, G&P 499, S&S#1 161, VU
    467

Put peace into each other's hands, BOP 560, MV 173

Seed, scattered and sown, CBWIII 604, G&P 516

Sent forth by God's blessing, BOP 775, G&P 588, VU 481

Thou, who at thy first Eucharist didst pray, BOP 559, CP 57

We are one, as we come, VU402

We gather here, in Jesus' name, VU 469

1. Kindle in Us the Desire

Orientation

This ecumenical prayer service is offered as prayer to God and meditation, asking God to purify and deepen in the Christian faithful the *very desire for Christian reconciliation and unity.* If the unity of Christ's Body, the Church, is according to the will of God and the prayer of Jesus, then the growth of such desire must also be according to the will of God — and this, despite misgivings, fears, lingering prejudices, insufficient mutual knowledge. This prayer service is intended to help us seek the *grace* of the *desire* for Christian unity.

ORDER OF SERVICE

Gathering Song
(choose appropriate hymn or instrumental)

Greeting

Presider: May the one God and Father of all, who is above all and through all and in all, be with you.

All: May we rejoice in the one body, the one Spirit, the one hope of our calling, one Lord, one faith, one baptism to the glory of God. Amen. (cf. Eph. 4: 1-6)

(informal welcome)

Roll Call Ritual

Reader 1: We have come to the house of the Lord,

R2:	gathered from the parishes/congregations of . . . and . . .
	or
	members of . . . (name denominations present)
All:	**Thanks be to God!**

Gloria[*]

| P: | Glory to God in the highest |
| All: | **And peace to God's people on earth.** |

| P: | Lord God, heavenly King, almighty God and Father, |
| All: | **We worship you, we give you thanks.** |

| P: | We praise you for your glory. |
| All: | **Lord Jesus Christ, only Son of the Father.** |

| P: | Lord God, Lamb of God, |
| All: | **You take away the sin of the world: have mercy on us;** |

P:	You take away the sin of the world: receive our prayer.
All:	**You are seated at the right hand of the Father: have mercy on us.**
P:	For you alone are the holy one,
All:	**You alone are the Lord,**

| P: | You alone are the Most High: Jesus Christ, with the Holy Spirit, |
| All: | **In the glory of God the Father. Amen.** |

---

* "The Lima Liturgy," in *Eucharistic Worship in Ecumenical Contexts*, Ed. Thomas F. Best and Dagmar Heller, WCC Publications, Geneva, 1998, p. 52, n. 6.

Prayer*

P: O faithful God, we know that to believe in Christ
       means to desire unity, to desire unity means to desire
       the communion of grace found in your Son's Body,
       the Church. We humbly ask you for the grace to desire
       reconciliation and unity among all Christians, costly
       though this grace be. We make this prayer through the
       same Jesus Christ, our Lord, in the unity of the Holy
       Spirit.

All: **Amen.**

LITURGY OF THE WORD

First Reading Eph 4: 1-6, "there is one Lord, one faith"

Meditative Psalm
(may be read or sung responsively)

Psalm 127 "Unless the Lord builds the house . . ."

Gospel Acclamation

P: Rejoicing in the real yet imperfect communion which
       joins us together,

All: **let us hear the Gospel!**

P: Journeying together toward full visible communion,

All: **let us harken to God's word and will!**

Gospel Reading Matthew 11: 25-30

(moment of silence)

---

* Inspired by *Ut Unum Sint*, Pope John Paul II, Encyclical Letter on
  Commitment to Ecumenism, 1995, n. 9b.

Sermon/Homily
(offered by one person, or shared by two persons in dialogue)

Profession of faith *(optional)*
The Apostles' Creed

Intercessory Prayers
(the presider introduces the prayers)

Reader: Giving thanks for the real yet imperfect communion that joins Christians together, we pray:

All: **Come, Holy Spirit of reconciliation and unity; come and renew the face of the Church, for the sake of God's world.**

R: That the unity of the Church may be healed and strengthened, we pray:

All: **Come, Holy Spirit . . . (as above)**

R: That the Holy Spirit would kindle in us the desire for unity in diversity, through the conversion of hearts, we pray:

All: **Come, Holy Spirit . . .**

R: That the Holy Spirit would remove all fears, prejudices and lukewarmness, we pray:

All: **Come, Holy Spirit . . .**

R: That we may all be led and encouraged into the purification of past memories, we pray:

All: **Come, Holy Spirit...**

R: For steadfast faith, hope and love on the demanding road ahead for the Churches, we pray:

All: Come, Holy Spirit . . .

The Lord's Prayer (*together*)

Prayer and Greeting of Peace

P: Peace be with you, prophets,
peace be with you, apostles,
and peace be with you, martyrs,
who loved the Lord of peace;
and peace be with the holy church
in which dwell the sons and daughters of peace.[*]

The peace of the Lord be with you.

All: **And also with you.**

P: Let us offer each other a sign of peace.

(The peace greeting is shared.)

Closing prayer

P: Let us pray.

All: **O God of the new and eternal covenant in Christ, we give you thanks for the gift of prayer and we beg you, yet again, to kindle in us a strong and effective desire for Christian unity, as Christ wills it, and by the means he wills. We make this prayer through the same Christ our Lord. Amen.**

Final Blessing and Sending forth[†]

---

[*] Vesper hymn, Syrian liturgy, drawn from *Let Us Pray to the Lord*, A Collection of Prayers from the Eastern and Oriental Orthodox Traditions, Ed. by Georges Lemopoulos, WCC Publications, Geneva, p. 59.

[†] *Ut unum sint*, Pope John Paul II, Encyclical Letter on *Commitment to Ecumenism*, 1995, n. 103a.

P: The Lord be with you.
All: **And also with you.**

P: Mend your ways, encourage one another, live in
        harmony, and the God of love and peace will be with
        you. (cf. 2 Cor. 13: 11)
All: **Thanks be to God!**

Closing hymn
(suitable hymn, or instrumental music)

2. Jesus Christ:
God's "Yes" to Us and Our "Amen" to God

Orientation

This service proposes prayer and meditation on the *gift of authority* in the one Church of Christ. We ask God for wisdom, humility and courage regarding this difficult issue among the churches. The substance of this ecumenical prayer format is drawn from *The Gift of Authority* (Authority in the Church III), an agreed statement by the Anglican-Roman Catholic International Commission (1998). Thus this prayer service is particularly fitting for common prayer between Anglicans and Roman Catholics, while remaining a worthy source of meditation and common prayer for all Christian denominations.

Preparation

Learn and rehearse songs, as warranted. Prepare basin, pitcher with water and towel — or 2 of each — on side table.

ORDER OF SERVICE

Gathering Song

Greeting

Presider: The grace of our Lord Jesus Christ, the love of God, and the communion of the Holy Spirit be with you all.

All: **And also with you.**

Call to Worship[*]

P: For as the heavens are higher than the earth, so are my ways higher than your ways and my thoughts than your thoughts.

All: **As the rain and snow come down from heaven and do not return until they have watered the earth, making it to blossom and bear fruit, to give seed for sowing and bread to eat,**

P: so shall the word that comes from my mouth prevail; it shall not return to me fruitless without accomplishing my purpose or succeeding in the task I give it (Is. 55). Rejoicing in the real yet imperfect communion which joins us together,

All: **we give thanks to God!**

P: Journeying together toward full visible communion,

All: **Lord, have mercy!**

Kyrie, eleison (*sung*)

Prayer

P: O faithful God, you sent your beloved Son, Jesus, into the world as the one in whom all your promises find their "Yes." Help us, in the power of the Holy Spirit, to overcome our divisions, so that together we may say and live a united "Amen" to your glory. This we ask, through Jesus Christ our Lord.

All: **Amen.**

---

* *Service of the Word,* developed under the auspices of the Lutheran-Roman Catholic Bishops Annual Meeting sponsored by Lutheran World Ministries and the National Conference of Catholic Bishops' Committee for Ecumenical and Interreligious Affairs (USA), 1986.

LITURGY OF THE WORD

First Reading 2 Cor. 1: 18-20, "In him it is always 'Yes.'"

(Silent reflection)

Reader: "Therefore, since it is by God's mercy that we are engaged in this ministry,

All: **we do not lose heart . . .**

R: But we have this treasure in clay jars, so that it may be made clear

All: **that this extraordinary power belongs to God and does not come from us."** (2 Cor. 4: 1-7)

and/or

Alleluia Acclamation

Gospel   Lk. 22: 24-27, "But I am among you as one who serves."

Sermon/Homily*
(presented by one person, or shared by two persons in dialogue)
(moment of silence)

Mutual washing of hands or feet

(The leader(s) in the prayer service, as well as one or two pairs of persons from the assembly, take part in this ritual. Mutual washing is done in pairs (this rite, to be done well, should be rehearsed in advance). The following quotations from Scripture are recited chorally, at measured pace, and may be repeated for the duration of the rite.)

---

*   Please consult *Suggestions for homilists/preachers regarding bilateral sermons/homilies.*

Side 1:	"So if I, your Lord and Teacher, have washed your feet,
Side 2:	**you also ought to wash another's feet.**

Side 1:	For I have set you an example,
Side 2:	**that you also should do as I have done to you"** (Jn. 13: 14-15).

(a moment of silence, then start again: "So if . . .")

Hymn

Intercessory Prayers
(introduced by the presider)

R:	That God will lead us to the goal we desire, the healing of our divisions, so that together we may say a united "Amen" to the glory of God. (cf. 2 Cor.1:20)
All:	**Jesus Christ is God's "Yes" to humankind.**

R:	That the life-giving obedience of Jesus may call forth our own response of courageous obedience to God.
All:	**Jesus Christ is God's "Yes" to humankind.**

R:	That the faith of individual Christians may be rooted in, and strengthened by, the faith of their community.
All:	**Jesus Christ is God's "Yes" to humankind.**

R:	That the gift of authority may be faithfully exercised in all Christian communities, local and universal, so that the Church may grow in obedience to the Holy Spirit.
All:	**Jesus is indeed God's "Yes" to humankind.**

Our Father . . .

Greeting of Peace

P: Lord Jesus Christ, you said to your apostles: I leave you
        peace, my peace I give you. Look not on our sins, but
        on the faith of your Church, and grant us the peace
        and unity of your kingdom, where you live for ever and
        ever.

All: **Amen.**

P: Let us offer each other a sign of peace.

(The greeting of peace is shared.)

Closing prayer

P: O God, when the real yet imperfect communion
        between us becomes more visible, the web of unity,
        woven from communion with you and reconciliation
        with each other, is extended and strengthened:
        May the "Amen" we say to you, our one Lord, come
        more closely to being an "Amen" lived together by
        the one holy people witnessing to God's salvation
        and reconciling love in a broken world (cf. *Gift of
        Authority*, n. 63) We make this prayer through Christ
        our Lord.

All: **Amen.**

Final Blessing

P: The Lord be with you.
All: **And also with you.**

P: May almighty God bless you, the Father, Source of all
        being, and the Son, eternal Word, and the Holy Spirit.
All: **Amen, amen. Come, Lord Jesus!**

The Sending

P: Go, in the way of Christ!
All: **Amen, amen. Thanks be to God!**

Closing hymn
(choose hymn or instrumental piece)

3. Baptized in the One Lord

Orientation

This ecumenical service is focused on the *one baptism*, gift of the new Covenant and bond of unity for the disciples of the Lord. It is a celebration of thanksgiving, praise and rejoicing! In baptism we are all incorporated into the Body of Christ, and therefore re-born as true sisters and brothers in Jesus. Are we re-discovering our sisterhood and brotherhood in Christ? Let us remind ourselves that, in faithfulness to baptismal unity, we are called to, and graced for, full visible unity in the Body . . . overcoming barriers . . . or perceived barriers . . . united in witness, in mission, and around the table of the one Lord.

ORDER OF SERVICE

Gathering Song
(hymn or instrumental)

Greeting

Presider: May the one God and Father of all, who is above all and through all and in all, be with you.

All: **May we rejoice in the one body, the one Spirit, the one hope of our calling, one Lord, one faith, one baptism to the glory of God. Amen.** (cf. Ephesians 4: 1-6)

Roll Roll Call Ritual

Reader 1:   We have come to the house of the Lord,

R2:   gathered from the parishes/congregations of . . . and . . .

or

members of . . . (name denominations present)

All: **Thanks be to God!**

(This ritual is omitted when a single congregation/parish or denomination is using this prayer format.)

Words of welcome

Prayer[*]

P: Let us pray. Lord God, gracious and merciful, you anointed your Beloved Son with the Holy Spirit at his baptism in the Jordan, and you consecrated him prophet, priest and king; pour out your Spirit on us again that we may be faithful to our baptismal calling, ardently desire the communion of Christ's body and blood, and serve the poor of your people and all who need our love, through Jesus Christ, your Son, our Lord, who lives and reigns with you, in the unity of the Holy Spirit, world without end.

All: **Amen.**

LITURGY OF THE WORD
(the reading itself is choral)

First Reading Romans 6: 3-6.11, "baptized into Christ . . ."

Presider: Paul writes:

---

[*] "The Lima Liturgy," in *Eucharistic Worship in Ecumenical Contexts*, Ed. Thomas F. Best and Dagmar Heller, WCC Publications, Geneva, 1998, p. 52, n. 7.

Choir 1: "Do you not know that all of us who have been baptized into Christ Jesus were baptized into his death?

Choir 2: Therefore we have been buried in him by baptism, into death, so that, just as Christ was raised from the dead by the glory of the Father, so we too might walk in newness of life.

Choir 1: For if we have been united with him in a death like his, we will certainly be united with him in a resurrection like his.

Choir 2: We know that our old self was crucified with him so that the body of sin might be destroyed, and we might no longer be enslaved to sin.

Choir 1: So you also must consider yourselves dead to sin and alive to God in Christ Jesus."

All: **The word of the Lord!**

(*moment of silence*)

Gospel Acclamation[*]

Alleluia (*chanted*)

The following acclamation is read by one reader:

> When you, O Lord, were baptized in the Jordan, the worship of the Trinity was made manifest. For the voice of the Father bears witness to you, and called

---

[*] Adapted from *The Liturgikon, The Out-of-Doors Blessing of Water, The Apolytikion of Theophany, pp. 456-477,* The Antiochian Orthodox Christian Archdiocese of North America, 1989.

you his beloved Son. And the Spirit, in the likeness of a dove, confirmed the truthfulness of his word. O Christ, our God, who has revealed yourself and has enlightened the world, glory to you.

Alleluia, repeated

Gospel *Mark 10: 35-40, Jesus' own baptism*

Sermon/Homily
(brief preferably)

Ritual of water

P: *(prays the following blessing over the bowl of water)**

My brothers and sisters, let us ask God to bless this water, divinely created, which we shall use to recall our baptism. May God renew us and keep us faithful to the Spirit we have all received.

(moment of silence)

Lord our God, be with us as we recall the wonder of our creation and the greater wonder of our redemption. Bless this water: it makes the seed grow, it refreshes us and makes us clean. You have made of it a servant of your loving kindness: through water you set your people free, and quenched their thirst in the desert. With water the prophets announced a new covenant that you would make with humankind. By water, made holy by Christ in the Jordan, you made our sinful nature new in the bath that gives rebirth.

---

* Adapted from *Sacramentary, The Roman Missal* Canadian Catholic Conference, 1974, Easter Vigil, p. 267.

Let this water remind us of our baptism. We ask this
through Christ our Lord.

All: **Amen.**

(*A pitcher of water and some cups have been placed on a table in a
suitably prominent place; alongside the pitcher and cups, a large bowl
of water. The presider will invite people to come forward in pairs, dip
their hands in the bowl of water, experiencing the water prayerfully or
playfully. She/he will then invite them to move to the pitcher, where
they will pour cups of water for each other to drink.)**

P: You are invited to come forward in pairs, with a
brother or sister in the Lord, or with a child in the
congregation. Dip your hands into the bowl and
experience the gift of water prayerfully or playfully.
Sign yourselves with water, or not, according to your
tradition. Then, you are invited to share cups of water
from the pitcher, pouring the water for one another.
While you are seated, join together in singing . . .

(*While the ritual unfolds, or immediately after, a hymn is sung.*)

Profession of faith and re-commitment[†]

P: Do you believe in God who has created and is creating,
who has come in Jesus, the Word made flesh, to
reconcile and make us new, and who works in us and
others by the Spirit?

All: **I do, by the grace of God.**

---

[*] Drawn and adapted from *Worship Anthology, A Collection of Worship
Resources* contributed by the Churches of the Conference of Mennonite
Churches in Canada, Vol. I, 1995, Section III, p. 27.

[†] Drawn from *Celebrate God's Presence*, A Book of Services for the United
Church of Canada, United Church Publishing House, 2000, Renewal of Baptismal Faith, pp. 362-363.

P: Desiring the freedom of the new life in Christ, do you seek to resist evil, and to live in love and justice?

All: **I will, God being my helper.**

P: Will you follow the way of Jesus Christ?

All: **I will, God being my helper.**

Intercessory Prayers
(introduced by the presider)

Reader: In thanksgiving for our unity in baptism, in whose waters we truly become sisters and brothers reborn in Christ, we pray to the Lord.

All: **We give you thanks, O God.**

R: For the courage to constantly reaffirm our baptism and its implications for a life of discipleship together in truth and love, we pray to the Lord.

All: **Lord, have mercy.**

R: That churches may reconcile their understandings and practices regarding infant baptism and believer's baptism, we pray to the Lord.

All: **Lord, have mercy.**

R: That the churches may gather with one prophetic voice, proclaiming in deed and word God's command to share clean drinking water around the globe, we pray to the Lord.

All: **Lord, have mercy.**

R:	That, living baptism faithfully, we might be granted full visible communion around the one table of the Lord, we pray to the Lord.
All:	**Lord, have mercy.**

Our Father . . .

Greeting and Sharing of Peace

P:	May the reconciliation and peace of the one Lord be always with you.
All:	**And also with you.**

P:	Blessed are the peacemakers,
All:	**for they will be called children of God** (Mt. 5: 9).

P:	Let us share the peace of Christ.

(The peace is shared.)

Closing Prayer[*]

P:	Almighty and eternal God, you keep together those you have united. Look kindly on all who follow Jesus your Son. We are consecrated to you by our common baptism; make us one in the fullness of faith and keep us one in the fellowship of love. We make this prayer through Christ, our Lord.
All:	**Amen.**

---

[*] *Sacramentary, The Roman Missal,* Canadian Catholic Conference, 1974, p. 973.

Final Blessing and Sending Forth[*]

P: The grace of Christ attend you, the love of God surround you, the Holy Spirit keep you.

All: **Amen.**

P: All who are united in the covenant of baptism are the body of Christ in the world. Go in peace.

All: **Amen.**

Closing hymn (*or instrumental*)

---

[*] *Celebrate God's Presence — A Book of Services for the United Church of Canada*, United Church Publishing House, 2000, p. 368.

4. "Now justified by God's grace . . .
through faith in Jesus Christ."
(Romans 3: 24.22)

Orientation

This Prayer Service is a prayer of praise and thanksgiving centred on the good news of *our justification by the grace of God through faith in Jesus Christ.* More pointedly, the Service underscores and celebrates the journey of theological reconciliation accomplished by the Lutheran churches and the Roman Catholic Church on the doctrine of justification. We give thanks for the patient research and for the consensus arrived at by these churches of the West regarding fundamental truths of the doctrine of justification.

Excerpt from the *Joint Declaration on the Doctrine of Justification,* confirmed 31 October 1999:

n. 15 Together we confess: By grace alone, in faith in Christ's saving work and not because of any merit on our part, we are accepted by God and receive the Holy Spirit, who renews our hearts while equipping and calling us to good works.

ORDER OF SERVICE

Gathering Song
(choose an appropriate hymn or instrumental prelude)

(Leaders in the service process to their places, or simply gather at their places.)

Greeting

Presider: May the God of mercy who justifies us by faith in Jesus Christ, through grace, be with you,

All: **and with your spirit.**

(words of welcome)

Call to Worship[*]

P: For as the heavens are higher than the earth, So are my ways higher than your ways and my thoughts than your thoughts.

All: **As the rain and snow come down from heaven and do not return until they have watered the earth, making it to blossom and bear fruit, to give seed for sowing and bread to eat,**

P: so shall the word that comes from my mouth prevail; it shall not return to me fruitless without accomplishing my purpose or succeeding in the task I give it (Is. 55).

(slight pause)

Rejoicing in the real yet imperfect communion that joins us together,

All: **we give thanks to God!**

P: Journeying together toward full visible fellowship,
All: **Lord, have mercy.**

Penitential rite

Reader: So if I, your Lord and Teacher, have washed your feet,
All: **you also ought to wash one another's feet.**

R: For I have set you an example,

---

[*]   *Service of the Word,* developed under the auspices of the Lutheran-Roman Catholic Bishops Annual Meeting sponsored by Lutheran World Ministries and the National Conference of Catholic Bishops' Committee for Ecumenical and Interreligious Affairs (USA), 1986.

All:	**that you also should do as I have done to you.** (Jn. 13: 14-15)

(pause)

R :	So when you are offering your gift at the altar,
All :	**if you remember that your brother or sister has something against you,**

R :	leave your gift before the altar and go;
All :	**first be reconciled to your brother or sister,**

R :	and then come and offer your gift. (Mt. 5: 23-24)

(pause)

R :	Why do you see the speck in your neighbour's eye,
All :	**but do not notice the log in your own eye?**

R :	Or how can you say to your neighbour,
All :	**"Let me take the speck out of your eye,"**

R :	while the log is in your own eye?
All :	**You hypocrite, first take the log out of your own eye,**

R :	and then you will see clearly
All :	**to take the speck out of your neighbour's eye** (Mt. 7: 3-5).

(pause)

Prayer

P:	O merciful God, our hearts are broken and our spirits numbed, as we recall the prejudices, offensive words,

harsh reproaches, and hostile attitudes levelled by Catholics and Protestants against each other, for many centuries, over the doctrine of justification by faith through grace. Again and again we ask your forgiveness . . .

All: . . . and each other's forgiveness.

P: We beg your mercy, the purifying presence of your Spirit of holiness and the healing of painful memories. This we ask, through Jesus Christ, our Lord.

All: Amen.

Greeting of Peace

P: The God of peace be with you all (Rom. 15:33).

All: Amen.

(Presider invites members of the assembly to exchange a greeting of peace.)

LITURGY OF THE WORD

Reading

Ephesians 2: 4-10, 13-22 "by grace you have been saved"

(Reading done by two readers, woman and man, or two youths, if possible.)

Sermon/Homily *(bilateral if suitable)**

(moment of silence)

---

* This short sermon/homily could be delivered by two persons. Please consult *Suggestions for homilists/preachers regarding bilateral sermons/homilies.*

Hymn

Intercessions
(Presider introduces the prayer intentions.)

Reader: In thanksgiving for the unfathomable mystery of Christ unfolding in the universe, throughout all ages,

All: **thanks be to God!**

R: I In praise and thanksgiving for the undeserved gift of our justification through Jesus Christ,

All: **thanks be to God!**

R: That the Church, and the churches, be a faithful sign and instrument of God's loving purpose in the world,

All: **we pray to the Lord.**

R: That the Holy Spirit would kindle our desire for full unity in diversity, through a change of hearts,

All: **we pray to the Lord.**

(Presider concludes the intercessions.)

(an offering may be taken up)

The Lord's Prayer
(The presider invites the congregation to pray, each in one's own language.)

The Peace

Closing Prayer[*]

P: Lord, hear the prayers of your people and bring the hearts of believers together in your praise and in common sorrow for our sins. Heal all divisions among Christians that we may rejoice in the perfect unity of your Church and move together as one to eternal life in your kingdom. We ask this, through Jesus Christ, our Lord.

All: **Amen.**

Blessing and Sending Forth

P: The Lord be with you.

All: **And also with you.**

P: Mend your ways, encourage one another, live in harmony, and the God of love and peace will be with you. (cf. 2 Cor. 13: 11)

Closing hymn
(hymn, or instrumental only)

---

[*]   *Sacramentary, The Roman Missal,* Canadian Catholic Conference, 1974, p. 975.

5. Healing of Memories — Forgiveness

Orientation

This prayer service or liturgy focuses on the need for the churches and individual Christians to receive from the Holy Spirit the on-going grace of healing of memories through forgiveness. This is a necessary *conversion* step if the churches are to overcome their divisions and mutual estrangement.[*]

Preparation

Place a fire-safe dish (bowl or pan) on a small side table for the burning of some crumpled slips of paper. Have matches or a lighter ready.

ORDER OF SERVICE

Instrumental Prelude

(Leaders in the service process in or simply gather at their places.)

---

[*] International Reformed-Roman Catholic dialogue, *Towards a Common Understanding of the Church*, 1990, nn. 62-63:

"The result is that today, as in the past, the same words, even the same biblical expressions, are sometimes received and understood by us in quite different ways.

"The very recognition that thus is the case marks important progress in our attempt to rid our memories of significant resentments and misconceptions. We need to set ourselves more diligently, however, to the task of reconciling these memories, by writing together the story of what happened in the16th century."

Mennonite World Conference-Catholic Church international dialogue, *Called Together to Be Peacemakers* 2003, n. 192:

"The healing of memories requires, first of all, a purification of memories. This involves facing those difficult events of the past that give rise to divergent interpretations of what happened and why . . . . A purification of memory includes an effort to purge 'from personal and collective conscience all forms of resentment or violence left by the inheritance of the past on the basis of a new and rigorous historical-theological judgment, which becomes the foundation for a renewed moral way of acting'. (*Memory and Reconciliation*, 5.1.) On this basis, both Catholics and Mennonites have the possibility of embarking on a sure and trustworthy way of thinking about and relating to each other that is in accordance with Christian love (cf. 1 Cor. 13)."

Call to worship (*stand*)
Psalm 95

Presider: Come, let us sing to the Lord and shout with joy to the Rock who saves us.

All: **Let us approach him with praise and thanksgiving and sing joyful songs to the Lord.**

P: Come, then, let us bow down and worship, bending the knee before the Lord, our maker.

All: **For he is our God and we are his people, the flock he shepherds.**

P: Today, listen to the voice of the Lord: do not grow stubborn, as your fathers did in the wilderness,

All: **when at Meriba and Massah they challenged me and provoked me, although they had seen all my works.**

(informal welcome)

Hymn of Praise

Opening prayer

P: God of mercy and forgiveness, we thank you for the fellowship, real yet imperfect, that unites the disciples and churches of your Son. Yet we also beg you to grant churches the healing of memories they need, through reconciliation and mutual forgiveness. Lord Jesus, healer of broken humanity, come and heal us, in the power of your Spirit. Come, Lord Jesus!

All: **Amen.**

LITURGY OF THE WORD

Entrance of the Word (with procession and singing)

(A procession moves from the back to the front of the church/
sanctuary; it can include, very simply, the book-bearer preceded
by two candle-bearers walking together; the lectionary (or Bible)
is placed in a central and worthy place, the candles placed at
its sides. During the procession an "Alleluia" is sung, including
this verse (chanted or recited): "Not seven times, but, I tell you,
seventy-seven times." Mt.18: 22)

(moment of silence)

Gospel Proclamation (*seated*)

(This is a sequential reading of five short New Testament texts,
proclaimed by five readers located in five different locations in
the worshipping area; readings to be proclaimed without title
or chapter and verse, at measured pace, by the readers standing
and facing the assembly from their places; a 5-second interval of
silence between readings should be observed.)

1. 1 Corinthians 5: 7
2. Colossians 3: 13-15
3. Matthew 5: 23-24
4. Matthew 18: 21-22
5. Mark 1: 40-41 (in part)

"'If you choose, you can make me clean.'
Moved with pity, Jesus stretched out his hand . . .
. . . 'I do choose. Be made clean!'"

(longer moment of silence)

Homily/Sermon[*]
(moment of silence)

The Two Questions

(Participants are invited by the presider(s) to write their responses on the small slips of paper distributed before the service. Time is given. Papers are then gathered by passing collection baskets. The collected pieces of paper are then burned, at the front, in a suitable (safe) container. This is done in silence.)

1. Asking Forgiveness

Please write down *one thing* that you or your church (especially if you are a church leader) would want to ask forgiveness for, from God and from another church, or member of another church . . . (e.g., "I wish to ask forgiveness for . . . my pointed jokes at . . . my arrogance toward . . . my church's indifference to other churches . . . etc.")

2. Healing of Memories

One specific memory or prejudice I confess to God, and beg to be healed from: (e.g. "my ignorant prejudice regarding . . . a hurt or offense my Church suffered from another church . . . my own memory of a painful . . .")

Hymn

Intercessions
(The presider introduces the petitions)

---

[*] This short sermon/homily may be delivered by two persons. Please see *Suggestions for homilists/preachers regarding bilateral sermons/homilies."* In this Prayer Service, it is suggested that the sermon time be spent in a brief dual explanation of the *two questions* which participants will be invited to respond to, immediately after the homily.

Reader:	For the consolation and spiritual renewal of all the churches, we pray to the Lord.
All:	**Kyrie eleison** (*sung, as after each of the following three pleadings*)

R:	For the healing of the collective memory of each church regarding our divided past, we pray . . .
All:	**Kyrie eleison**

R:	For the healing of memories through the purification of hearts, we pray . . .
All:	**Kyrie eleison**

R:	For the healing of memories through mutual forgiveness, we pray . . .
All:	**Kyrie eleison**

Presider:	Faithful God, we urgently implore your forgiveness and we beseech the gift of a repentant heart, so that all Christians, reconciled with you and with one another, will be able, in one body and in one spirit, to experience anew the joy of full communion.[*]
All:	**Amen.**

Lord's Prayer
(The presider invites each one to pray in his/her own language.)

The Peace

P:	Let the peace of Christ rule in your hearts
All:	**to which indeed we were called in the one body** (Col. 3:15).

(The presider invites the assembly to share the peace of Christ.)

---

[*] *Called Together to be Peacemakers*, n. 200.

Benediction[*]

P: May the love of God enfold us.
All: **May the grace of God uphold us.**

P: May the power of God set us free
All: **to love and serve all God's people.**

P: Now to God, who by means of the power working in us, is able to do so much more than we can ask or even think; to God be glory in the church and in Christ Jesus for all times, for ever and ever.
All: **Amen.**

Sending forth

P: Go in the healing and peace of Christ.
All: **Thanks be to God!**

Closing hymn
(suitable hymn, or instrumental)

---

* *Worshipping Ecumenically*, Ed. by Per Harling, World Council of Churches 1995, p. 33.

6. "For the Conversion of the Churches"

Orientation

This prayer service is focused on the call to all churches to undergo some form(s) of Christian *conversion*. As human beings we are all sinners, and as institutions the churches are subject to sin and distortions in varied guise, insofar as they are human. Hence, *"ecclesia semper reformanda"* – the church always in need of being reformed. Humility and prayer certainly help the churches see more clearly where and how they are called to conversion, as well as the superabundant grace offered.

- "This requirement of conversion is therefore an invitation to our *confessional identities* to open up to each other and let themselves be penetrated by the values which the others bear. In particular, each confession must ask itself if its judgment of the others is really founded on the gospel." (Taken from the document: *For the Conversion of the Churches* published by the ecumenical dialogue group, *Groupe des Dombes,* 1991, in English translation, WCC Publications 1993, n. 48.)
- "But friendly division is still division. We must not let our present division be seen as normal, as the natural expression of a Christian marketplace with churches representing different options for a variety of spiritual tastes. Consumerist values and an ideology of diversity can anesthetize us to the wound of division. Recovering from this ecumenical anesthesia is one of the strongest present challenges to faithfulness." (Taken from the ecumenical document: *In One Body Through the Cross — The Princeton Proposal for Christian Unity,* 2003, n. 44.)
- "There can be no ecumenism worthy of the name without interior conversion." (Taken from Vatican II, *Decree on Ecumenism,* 1964, n. 7.)

Instrumental Prelude

(Leaders in the service process in to their places, or simply gather at their places.)

Call to worship* *(stand)*

Presider: For as the heavens are higher than the earth, so are my ways higher than your ways and my thoughts than your thoughts.

All: **As the rain and snow come down from heaven and do not return until they have watered the earth, making it to blossom and bear fruit, to give seed for sowing and bread to eat,**

P: so shall the word that comes from my mouth prevail; It shall not return to me fruitless without accomplishing my purpose or succeeding in the task I give it (Is. 55).

All: **Rejoicing in the real yet imperfect communion which joins us together, we give thanks to God!**

P: Journeying together toward full visible communion,
All: **Lord, have mercy!**

(words of welcome)

Hymn of Praise

Penitential Rite

Reader 1: A reading from a commentary on the Lord's Prayer, by Saint Cyprian, bishop of Carthage, mid-3rd century:

---

* *Service of the Word*, developed under the auspices of the Lutheran-Roman Catholic Bishops Annual Meeting sponsored by Lutheran World Ministries and the National Conference of Catholic Bishops' Committee for Ecumenical and Interreligious Affairs (USA), 1986.

R2:	"God does not accept the sacrifice of a sower of division, but commands that he depart from the altar so that he may first be reconciled with his brother.
R1:	For God can be appeased only by prayers that make peace. To God, the better offering is peace, brotherly concord and a people made one in the unity of the Father, Son and Holy Spirit."

(moment of silence)

(The following invocations could be sung:)

P:	Kyrie, eleison
All:	**Kyrie, eleison**
P:	Christe, eleison
All:	**Christe, eleison**
P:	Kyrie, eleison
All:	**Kyrie, eleison**
P:	Gracious God, have mercy upon us, forgive us our sins and transform us so that we may live united in your love; through our Saviour Jesus Christ.
All:	**Amen.**

Greeting of peace

P:	Peace to all of you who are in Christ (1 Pet. 5:14).
All:	**And with your spirit.**

(The presider invites members of the assembly to share the peace)

Prayer

P: Faithful God, we give you thanks for calling us into the fellowship of your Son, Jesus Christ our Lord (cf. 1 Cor. 1: 9). Yet we also beg you, in fear and trepidation, to grant us the costly grace of conversion, for all our churches, our institutions and attitudes. Put in us your Spirit and a new heart, and lead us to greater faithfulness in seeking reconciliation and full communion. We ask this in the name of Jesus Christ, your Son and the Lord of the Church.

All: **Amen.**

LITURGY OF THE WORD

Entrance of the Word (*procession with singing*)

(A procession moves from the back to the front of the church/ sanctuary; it can include, very simply, the book-bearer preceded by two candle-bearers walking together; the lectionary (or Bible) is placed in a central and worthy place, with the candles at each side. During the procession an Alleluia *is sung, including this verse: "but when one turns to the Lord, the veil is removed" (2 Cor. 3:16).*

(moment of silence)

Gospel proclamation
Philippians 2: 1-11

(Responsively, verse by verse)

Sermon/homily*

---

* This short sermon/homily may be delivered by two persons. Please see *Suggestions for homilists/preachers regarding bilateral sermons/homilies.*

(moment of silence)

Hymn

Meditation

(from Homilies on First Corinthians, St. John Chrysostom, 4th century)[*]

P: Let there be no gap between us and Christ.
All: **For if there is any gap, immediately we perish.**

P: For the building stands because it is cemented together.
All: **Let us not then merely keep hold of Christ,**

P: but let us be cemented to him.
All: **Let us cleave to him by our works.**

P: He is the head,
All: **we are the body.**

P: He is the foundation,
All: **we the building.**

P: He is the vine,
All: **we the branches.**

P: He is the bridegroom,
All: **we the bride.**

P: He is the shepherd,
All: **we the sheep.**

---

[*] From materials distributed by the WCC, 2005.

P:	He is the way,
All:	**we walk in it.**

P:	Again, we are the temple,
All:	**he the indweller.**

P:	He is the only begotten,
All:	**we the brothers and sisters.**

P:	He is the heir,
All:	**we the heirs together with him.**

P:	He is the life,
All:	**we the living.**

P:	He is the resurrection,
All:	**we those who rise again.**

P:	He is the light,
All:	**we the enlightened.**

(a collection may be taken up)

The Lord's Prayer

(The presider invites all to pray, each in their own language.)

Blessing

P:	Sisters and brothers, in the words of Paul: "Mend your ways, encourage one another, live in harmony, and the God of love and peace will be with you.
All:	**Amen.**

| P: | The grace of the Lord Jesus Christ and the love of God and the fellowship of the Holy Spirit be with you all." (2 Cor. 13:11,13) |
| All: | **Thanks be to God!** |

Sending Forth[*]

| P: | Go out into the world in the power of the Holy Spirit to fulfill your high calling as disciples of Jesus Christ. |
| All: | **Amen!** |

Closing hymn
(or instrumental postlude)

---

[*] *Celebrate God's Presence — A Book of Services for The United Church of Canada*, United Church Publishing House, 2000, p. 73.

7. In the Hope of Full Communion
Around the Table of the Lord*

Orientation

The aim and hope of this Service is to enable fervent listening to the Word, and prayer, around the supreme blessing, and notoriously difficult issue, of the Eucharist/Holy Communion/Lord's Supper/ the Mass — in the present fellowship, real though imperfect, of the churches. Our hope is that churches and individual Christians will risk "gathering together" to pray this prayer, in humility and simplicity of heart. The two following Gathering Reflections are offered as preparation for worship (for silent reading and prayerful reflection in the Spirit of reconciliation and hope):

> The very celebration of the Eucharist is an instance of the Church's participation in God's mission to the world. This participation takes everyday form in the proclamation of the Gospel, service of the neighbour, and faithful presence in the world. As it is entirely the gift of God, the Eucharist brings into the present age a new reality which transforms Christians into the image of Christ, and therefore makes them his effective witnesses. . . . As it becomes one people, sharing the meal of the one Lord, the Eucharistic assembly must be concerned for gathering also those who are at present beyond its visible limits, because Christ invited to his feast all for whom he died. Insofar as Christians cannot unite in full fellowship around the same table to eat the same loaf and drink from the same cup, their missionary witness is weakened at both the individual and the corporate levels.
> (*Baptism, Eucharist and Ministry*, Faith and Order Paper No. 111. World Council of Churches, Geneva, 1982, Eucharist 25-26).

---

* This Prayer Service was drafted jointly by Rev. Ron McConnell of the United Church of Canada, and Rev. Bernard de Margerie, Roman Catholic priest, both from Saskatoon, Saskatchewan, Canada. The Service may appear difficult in more ways than one . . . Reading is also difficult . . . And all is grace!

Progress toward the unity Christ wills for his disciples, by the means he wills, urges us forward to deeper discernment and obedience in the ways of the Spirit. Let us encourage one another, learn to carry each other's burdens, and wash each other's feet, across denominational lines, so that we may "all be one" (John 17) for the credibility of our common mission in Christ, and for the glory of God in his reconciling grace (*Pastoral Directives for Sacramental Sharing*, Roman Catholic Diocese of Saskatoon, 2007, n. 24).

ORDER OF SERVICE

Instrumental prelude

(Leaders in the Service process to, or simply gather at, their places. There are two co-presiders and two readers.)

Greeting

Presider 1: May the one God and Father of all, who is above all and through all and in all, be with you.

All: **May we rejoice in the one body, the one Spirit, the one hope of our calling, one Lord, one faith, one baptism to the glory of God. Amen.** (cf. Eph. 4: 1-6)

(words of welcome)

Hymn of Entrance

Confession

P1   Have mercy on us, O God, according to your steadfast love . . . You desire truth in the inward being; therefore teach us wisdom in our secret heart (cf. Ps. 51: 1, 6).

P2   For failing to love and serve one another, as your disciples, across denominational lines, over the centuries and unto these times.

All **Grant to us, O Lord, a heart renewed, re-create in us your own spirit, Lord.**

P2 For our neglect and benign indifference toward the unity of your Church, which is your prayer and your will, O Lord.

All **Grant to us, O Lord, a heart renewed, re-create in us your own spirit, Lord.**

P2 For the waves of prejudice, un-Christian attitudes and words, all hurts inflicted or received, over the centuries, around the God-given gift of the Table of the Lord,

All **Grant to us, O Lord, a heart renewed, re-create in us your own spirit, Lord.**

Extending Peace*

P1 Love one another. As I have loved you, so you are to love one another. The Peace of Christ be with you all (Jn. 15: 12).

All **And with your spirit.**

P1 Let us offer one another signs of reconciliation and love.

Prayer†

P2 O God, whose Word is sharper than any two-edged sword, piercing both heart and conscience with many

---

* *Celebrate God's Presence*, A Book of Services for The United Church of Canada, 2000, p. 48.

† *United Church of Canada Service Book*, 1968.

wounds: let the sword of the Spirit pierce us through, and grant that the wounds inflicted by your truth may be healed by your love, through Jesus Christ our Lord

All   **Amen.**

LITURGY OF THE WORD

Entrance of the Word *(procession with singing)*

(A procession moves from the back to the front of the church/ sanctuary; it can include, very simply, the book-bearer carrying the Bible or lectionary preceded by two candle-bearers walking together; the lectionary (or Bible) is placed in a central place, lit candles at each side)

(During the procession a brief song or acclamation is sung, in honour of the Word; it might possibly include the verse "but when one turns to the Lord, the veil is removed" (2 Cor. 3:16)

First Reading   R1:   1 Corinthians 12: 12-14, 26-27
"Now you are the body of Christ and individually members of it"

Gospel Acclamation
(A refrain, an alleluia or other acclamation, is sung)

Gospel R2: John 21: 15-17
"Feed my sheep."

(moment of silence)

Hymn

Homily/Sermon*

---

* The sermon/homily may be delivered by two persons (of different

(moment of silence)

Acknowledging brokenness; Proclaiming our hope for full Communion in the Body of Jesus Christ Our Lord

- Two members [**R1** and **R2**] of the gathered community come forward (reflecting our diversity, divisions, and longed-for unity)
- They move to a table at the front of the church/sanctuary where a loaf of bread (preferably made of whole grains) has been placed on a table from the beginning of the Service, in good view of the congregation; it would be good if the loaf, when at rest, were placed on a plate on the table, within a sketched crown of thorns, thus linking visually the Bread with the Sacrifice of Christ.
- **R1** and **R2,** together, lift the plate with the loaf of bread and carry it forward to stand with the two presiders [**P1** and **P2**].
- **R1, R2, P1** and **P2,** together, gather around the table, holding the loaf of bread, while facing the congregation.

R1:   The Church receives the eucharist as a gift from the Lord (from *Baptism, Eucharist and Ministry*, Eucharist 1).

P1:   St. Paul wrote: "I have received from the Lord what I also delivered to you, that the Lord Jesus on the night when he was betrayed, took bread, and when he had given thanks, he broke it, and said: 'This is my body, which is for you. Do this in remembrance of me.'

R2:   In the same way also the cup, after supper, saying: 'This cup is the new covenant in my blood. Do this, as often as you drink it, in remembrance of me'" (1 Cor. 11: 23-25).

---

denominations) in dialogue. See the *Suggestions for homilists/preachers regarding bilateral homilies/sermons.*

(brief pause)

P2: They will hunger no more, and thirst no more, the sun will not strike them, nor any scorching heat;

All: **For the lamb at the centre of the throne will be their shepherd, and he will guide them to springs of the water of life, and God will wipe away every tear from their eyes.** (Rev. 7: 16-17)

R1, R2, P1, P2: This is the bread that came down from heaven,
(in unison) not like that which your ancestors ate, and they died. But the one who eats this bread will live for ever (Jn. 6: 58)

(moment of silence)

- After a moment, **P1** and **P2**, in a manner visible to the whole congregation, break/tear the bread into four distinct quarters, placing each quarter on a separate plate.
- **R1, R2, P1** and **P2** each carry one of the plates to a different corner of the assembly. The bread is then passed throughout the ranks of the gathered people so that each person is able to hold the plate and behold the bread for a moment, and then pass it on.
- Once all have held in prayerful reflection one of the quarter-loaves, **R1, R2, P1** and **P2** come forward from different directions (to reflect the longed-for coming together of God's people and God's Church from all corners of creation) each carrying a plate with a quarter-loaf to the front and stand together facing the congregation.
- **P1** and **P2**, in a manner visible to the whole assembly, fit the four broken pieces of the loaf of bread together again on a plate; the following is then said:

All: "For in the one Spirit we were all baptized into one body. . . . Now you are the body of Christ and individually members of it" (1 Cor. 12: 12, 27).

R1:   Blessed be the God and Father of our Lord Jesus Christ, who has blessed us in Christ with every spiritual blessing in the heavenly places (Eph. 1: 3).

P1:   For as often as you eat this bread and drink this cup, you proclaim the Lord's death until he comes (1 Cor. 11: 26).

R2:   And I will ask the Father, and he will give you another Advocate to be with you for ever. . . . You know him, because he abides in you, and he will help you. . . . (He) will teach you everything, and remind you of all that I have said to you (Jn. 14: 16, 17c, 26).

P2:   Lord, when was it that we saw you hungry and gave you food, or thirsty and gave you something to drink? And when was it that we saw you a stranger and welcomed you, or naked and gave you clothing? And when was it that we saw you sick or in prison and visited you?

All: Jesus said to them, "I am the bread of life. Whoever comes to me will never be hungry, and whoever believes in me will never be thirsty. . . . Those who eat my flesh and drink my blood abide in me, and I in them. Just as the living Father sent me, and I live because of the Father, so whoever eats me will live because of me (Jn. 6: 35, 56-57).

R1, R2, P1, P2: Truly I tell you, just as you did it to one of the
(in unison) least of these who are members of my family, you did it
to me (Mt. 25: 40).

(moment of silence)

R1 *and* **R2** *move to the ambo (lectern)*

Prayers

P1 *introduces the intercessions*

R1: In praise and thanksgiving for the saving mystery of
your Son's holy death and resurrection,

All: **Gracious God, your kingdom come!**

R2: In praise and thanksgiving for having called us as
sisters and brothers in the fellowship of your Son, Jesus
Christ, our Lord (see 1 Cor. 1: 9).

All: **Gracious God, your kingdom come!**

R1: In praise and thanksgiving for the Eucharist, the Lord's
Supper, gift and seal of the new covenant entrusted to
your Church,

All: **Gracious God, your kingdom come!**

R2: That the Holy Spirit would help the churches, and
especially their leaders, to untie the "knots," theological
or other, which prevent full fellowship of the faithful at
the table of the Lord, we pray to the Lord.

All: **God, come to our assistance. Jesus, make haste to
help us.**

R1: For the healing of hurts felt by individual Christians,
on account of the factual, ongoing disunity between

churches, wounding and weakening the Body of Christ, we pray to the Lord.

All: **God, come to our assistance. Jesus, make haste to help us.**

R2: For the healing of hurts felt by many of the faithful on account of present exclusions at the table of the Lord, we pray to the Lord.

All: **God, come to our assistance. Jesus, make haste to help us.**

R1: For the strengthening of the churches' missionary witness, through God's merciful gift of full fellowship around the table of the Lord, we pray to the Lord.

All: **God, come to our assistance. Jesus, make haste to help us.**

P2 concludes the intercessions

Anthem/solo/instrumental *(optional)*

(An offering may be received)

The Lord's Prayer
P1 invites all to pray, each in their own language

Final commitment

P1: For the renewed and strengthened commitment of churches and individual Christians on behalf of reconciliation and unity in diversity.

All: **We will follow the way of Jesus Christ.**

P2: For God's special graces of wisdom and strength for all church leaders, present and future.

All:	**We will follow the way of Jesus Christ.**
P1:	For humility and patience on this gospel path,
All:	**We will follow the way of Jesus Christ.**

Benediction

P2:	May the God and Father of our Lord Jesus Christ, who has chosen and blessed you in Christ with every spiritual blessing, lead you to be holy and blameless before him in love (cf. Eph. 1: 3-4).
All:	**Thanks be to God!**

Closing Hymn

As the people leave (optional; the assembly will need to be instructed about the meaning of this final gesture) one, two, or three attendants stand near the church exits. As each person leaves, the following short dialogue takes place:

Attendant: We are one body . . .
Response: one body in Christ!

or

Attendant: Let us be reconciled . . .
Response: at the Table of Jesus!

8. "Called Together to be Peacemakers"*

Orientation

This Prayer Service was prepared in reference to the important ecumenical document *Called Together to Be Peacemakers*. The document reports on a five-year period of study, dialogue, and prayer in common by an international group officially appointed by the Mennonite and Roman Catholic denominations.

The purpose of this ecumenical prayer service is to rejoice in, and celebrate, the reconciliation process starting to move between two traditions of Christianity. We celebrate growth in reconciliation and fellowship! At the same time, we receive the document's call, echoing the gospel, to be "peacemakers together." Here is the concluding paragraph of the document:

> After having worked with each other over these five years, we, Catholic and Mennonite members of this dialogue, want to testify together that our mutual love for Christ has united us and accompanied us in our discussions. Our dialogue has fortified the common conviction that it is possible to experience reconciliation and the healing of memories. Therefore we beseech God to bestow divine grace upon us for the healing of past relationships between Mennonites and Catholics, and we thank God for present commitments to reconciliation within the body of Christ. Together we pray that God may bless this new relationship between our two families of faith, and that the Holy Spirit may enlighten and enliven us in our common journey on the path forward.

Thus, all churches can and ought to join in, make their own, and celebrate any and all steps in reconciliation, healing of memories

---

* Title of an ecumenical document, prepared by the officially appointed international dialogue group of the Mennonite and Roman Catholic denominations, 2003.

and growth in Christ-fellowship — wherever such grace is given and embraced.

Preparation: Learn and rehearse songs, as needed.

ORDER OF SERVICE

Instrumental Prelude

(Leaders in the service process to their places, or simply gather at their places.)

Greeting

Presider: Grace, mercy, and peace from God the Father and Christ Jesus our Lord. (1 Tim. 1:2)

All: **And with your spirit.**

(words of welcome)

Entrance Hymn

Confession

P: The Lord Jesus taught us: "So when you are offering your gift at the altar, and if you remember that your brother or sister has something against you,

All: *(slowly)* **leave your gift there before the altar and go; first be reconciled to your brother or sister, and then come and offer your gift"** (Mt. 5: 23-24).

P: May almighty God have mercy on us, forgive us our sins, and bring us to everlasting life.

All: **Amen.**

Extending Peace[*]

P: Lord Jesus Christ, you said to your apostles, I leave you peace, my peace I give you. Look not on our sins, but on the faith of your Church, and grant us the peace and unity of your kingdom where you live for ever and ever.

All: **Amen.**

P: The peace of the Lord be with you always.
All: **And also with you.**

P: Let us offer each other a sign of peace.

Prayer

P: God of all mercy, you call your Church, and each of the churches, to bear witness to the gospel of peace grounded in Jesus Christ. Help your people to be peacemakers in our time, both in the world and in the Church, for we yearn to be called your children. This we ask, through Christ, our Lord.

All: **Amen.**

LITURGY OF THE WORD

Entrance of the Word *(procession with singing)*

(A procession moves from the back to the front of the church/ sanctuary; it can include, very simply, the book-bearer carrying the bible or lectionary preceded by two candle-bearers walking together; the lectionary (or Bible) is placed in a central place, candles at each side. During the procession a brief song or acclamation is sung, in honour of the Word.)

---

*   *Sacramentary, The Roman Missal,* Canadian Catholic Conference, 1974, p. 975.

First Reading   Isaiah 2: 2-4

"they shall beat their swords into ploughshares"

Gospel Acclamation

(A refrain is sung — an alleluia or the acclamation: "Praise to you, Lord, King of eternal glory", and the verse: "The effect of righteousness will be peace" Is. 32:17).

Gospel Reading   Matthew 5: 1-12

"blessed are the peacemakers"

(moment of silence)

Hymn   "Make me a channel of your peace"
(Prayer of St. Francis)

Sermon/Homily*

(moment of silence)

Prayers

Presider *introduces the intercessions*

Reader: For the churches, we ask wisdom and courage to re-read their church history together; we pray to the Lord.

All: **For he is our peace!** (Ephesians 2:14)

R: For world and national governments, that they would promote and invest in the fair sharing and distribution of the world's resources, we pray to the Lord.

---

*   This short sermon/homily may be given by two persons. Please see *Suggestions for homilists/preachers regarding bilateral sermons/homilies.*

All:	**For he is our peace!**
R:	That the churches receive the grace of humility, to ask for and extend forgiveness for injuries and hurts between them, past and present, we pray to the Lord.
All:	**For he is our peace!**
R:	That Christians would join faith and evangelization with justice and peace-making in their witness, we pray to the Lord.
All:	**For he is our peace!**
R:	For local congregations and parishes, to be strong and credible advocates of justice and peace in their own social settings, we pray to the Lord.
All:	**For he is our peace!**

Presider concludes the intercessions

(A collection may be received.)

The Lord's Prayer

(The presider invites all to pray, each in their own language.)

Blessing

P:	Sisters and brothers, in the words of Paul, "Mend your ways, encourage one another, live in harmony, and the God of love and peace will be with you.
All:	**Amen.**
P:	The grace of the Lord Jesus Christ and the love of God and the fellowship of the Holy Spirit be with you all!" (2 Cor. 13: 11, 13).

All: **Thanks be to God!**

Sending Forth[*]

P: I heard the Lord saying, "Whom shall I send? Who will go for us?" (Is. 6: 8).

All: **Here am I! Send me.**

Closing Hymn
(or instrumental postlude)

---

[*] *Worshipping Ecumenically*, Ed. by Per Harling, WCC Publications, 1995, p. 149.

9. "Mary: Grace and Hope in Christ"[*]

Orientation

The aim of this Ecumenical Prayer Service is to celebrate in joyful
faith our ancient common Christian heritage surrounding Mary,
the mother of our Lord Jesus Christ. We want to "give thanks
to God for Mary, the mother of the Lord, who is one with us in
that vast community of love and prayer we call the communion
of saints" (*Mary: Grace and Hope in Christ*, Preface, para. d).
We also wish to ask forgiveness for un-Christian attitudes and
conflicts that have accumulated between the churches over the
centuries, concerning the place of Mary in church life and doctrine.
Finally, we ask the Holy Spirit to guide us all in patiently untying
the theological (or other) "knots" which prevent us, sadly and
incredibly, from being of one heart and soul (see Acts 4:32) in this
dimension of the Christian Tradition.

The service intends to be gentle and joyful, yet not superficial.

ORDER OF SERVICE

Instrumental Prelude

*(Leaders in the service process to their places, or simply gather at
their places.)*

Scripture Sentence

Presider: O magnify the Lord with me,
All: **let us exalt God's name together!** (Psalm 34:3)

---

[*] Title of an ecumenical document published in 2004, the work of the Anglican-
Roman Catholic International Commission (ARCIC). This Ecumenical Prayer
Service was drafted with the collaboration of Rev. Jan Bigland-Pritchard,
Director (2005-2011) of the Prairie Centre for Ecumenism, Saskatoon,
Saskatchewan, Canada.

Greeting

P: Grace to you and peace from God our Father and the
Lord Jesus Christ. (Romans 1:7)

All: **And with your spirit.**

(words of welcome)

Hymn of Entrance

Prayer for Mercy (*sung*)

Kyrie eleison (x 2)
Christe eleison (x 2)
Kyrie eleison (x 2)

Prayer

P: God our Father, we give you thanks and praise for the
pattern of grace and hope in Christ exemplified in the
life of Mary, mother of our Lord Jesus Christ. While
we acknowledge the fact that there is still considerable
disagreement about Mary among the churches, we
beg you, in earnest hope, to help us recover fellowship
around this gift of your grace, within the mystery of
Christ, the one mediator between God and humankind
(see 1 Tim. 2:5.6). We ask this through the same Christ
our Lord.

All: **Amen.**

LITURGY OF THE WORD

Litany of Scripture — Prayer for illumination*

P: O God, your Word is a lamp to our feet, and a light to our path. Give us grace to receive your truth in faith and love.

All: **Amen.**

(Two Readers will alternate the following readings, while remaining standing at their places in the assembly.)

R1:   The angel said to her, "Do not be afraid, Mary, for you have found favour with God. And now, you will conceive in your womb and bear a son, and you will name him Jesus. He will be great, and will be called the Son of the Most High . . ." (Lk. 1: 30-32)

Side 1:   **There is one mediator between God and humankind, Christ Jesus, himself human.**

S2:   **And his mother said: "Do whatever he tells you." (Jn. 2:5)**

(pause)

R2:   Then Mary said, "Here am I, the servant of the Lord; let it be with me according to your word."

S1:   **There is one mediator between God and humankind, Christ Jesus, himself human.**

S2:   **And his mother said: "Do whatever he tells you" (Jn. 2: 5**

---

* *Celebrate God's Presence*, A Book of Services for the United Church of Canada, 2000, p. 44

(pause)

R1: While they were there, the time came for her to deliver her child. And she gave birth to her firstborn son and wrapped him in bands of cloth, and laid him in a manger, because there was no place for them in the inn. (Lk. 2: 6-7)

S1: **There is one mediator between God and humankind, Christ Jesus, himself human.**

S2: **And his mother said: "Do whatever he tells you."**

(pause)

R2: Jesus and his disciples had also been invited to the wedding. When the wine gave out, the mother of Jesus said to him, "They have no wine." And Jesus said to her: "What concern is that to you and to me? My hour has not yet come." His mother said to the servants: "Do whatever he tells you." (Jn. 2:3-5)

S1: **There is one mediator between God and humankind, Christ Jesus, himself human.**

S2: **And his mother said: "Do whatever he tells you."**

(pause)

R1: When Jesus saw his mother and the disciple whom he loved standing beside her, he said to his mother, "Woman, here is your son." Then he said to the disciple, "Here is your mother." And from that hour the disciple took her into his own home (Jn. 19: 26-27)

S1: There is one mediator between God and humankind, Christ Jesus, himself human.

S2: And his mother said: "Do whatever he tells you."

(pause)

R2: Then they returned to Jerusalem from the mount called Olivet. . . . When they had entered the city, they went to the room upstairs where they were staying. . . . All these were constantly devoting themselves to prayer, together with certain women, including Mary the mother of Jesus, as well as his brothers. (Acts 1:12-14)

S1: There is one mediator between God and humankind, Christ Jesus, himself human.

S2: And his mother said: "Do whatever he tells you."
(moment of silence)

Hymn (*thoughtful, suitable*)

Sermon/Homily*

(time of silence)

Prayers

(The presider introduces the intercessions.)

R: In thanksgiving for the witness of Scripture and of the ancient common Christian tradition regarding Mary, the mother of the Lord, we pray to the Lord.

---

* This homily/sermon may be delivered by two persons in dialogue. See *Suggestions for homilists/preachers regarding bilateral homilies/sermons.*

All: **Lord, give us joy, and have mercy.**

R: Rejoicing in Mary's prophetic words "Surely, from now on all generations will call me blessed." (Luke 1:48)

All: **Lord, give us joy, and have mercy.**

R: Asking forgiveness for the real and perceived abuses surrounding doctrine and devotion to Mary, at various times in the history of the Church, and also for the loss of some positive aspects of devotion and the lessening of her place in the life of the Church, we pray to the Lord.

All: **Lord, give us joy, and have mercy.**

R: Asking forgiveness, from God and from each other, for the willful blindness, un-Christian attitudes and conflicts accumulated between churches along the centuries, regarding the place of Mary in church doctrine and life, we pray to the Lord.

All: **Lord, give us joy, and have mercy.**

R: Begging the Spirit of truth and love to inspire the churches in untying the theological "knots" we have inherited from the past, regarding Mary, we pray to the Lord.

All: **Lord, give us joy, and have mercy.**

R: That we would be led to imitate Mary, the loving, obedient and humble disciple of her Lord and Son, we pray to the Lord.

All: **Lord, give us joy, and have mercy.**

(The presider concludes the prayers.)

(An offering may be received.)

Peace

P: Love one another.
As I have loved you,
so you are to love one another.
The Peace of Christ be with you all. (Jn. 15:12)

All: **And also with you.**

P: Let us offer one another signs of reconciliation and love.[*]

The Lord's Prayer

(The presider invites all to pray, each in their own language.)

Closing Reflection[†]

R: Mary epitomizes such participation in the life of God. Her response was not made without profound questioning, and it issued in a life of joy intermingled with sorrow, taking her even to the foot of her son's cross. When Christians join in Mary's 'Amen' to the 'Yes' of God in Christ, they commit themselves to an obedient response to the Word of God, which leads to a life of prayer and service. Like Mary, they not only magnify the Lord with their lips: they commit themselves to serve God's justice with their lives (cf. Luke 1: 46-55).

Final Commission

P: The Lord be with you.

All: **And also with you.**

---

[*] *Celebrate God's Presence*, p. 48.
[†] *Mary: Grace and Hope in Christ*, Introduction, n.5.

P:	Lead a life worthy of the calling to which you have been called,
All:	**with all humility and gentleness,**
P:	with patience, bearing with one another in love,
All:	**making every effort to maintain the unity of the Spirit in the bond of peace** (Eph. 4:1-3).
P:	Go, in the peace of Christ!
All:	**Thanks be to God!**

Closing hymn
(*or instrumental postlude*)

10. Morning Prayer Together

Orientation

As Christians, disciples of the Lord, we are invited, indeed urged, to come together for prayer, beyond denominational boundaries. A new day has dawned, gift of God, who is Source of all being, a day enlightened by the risen Lord Jesus, light for our lives, a field of the Holy Spirit who transforms us in holiness. We gather for prayer, praising God, asking our merciful God to receive our lives as a living sacrifice, holy and acceptable, our spiritual worship (cf. Romans 12: 1).

We also implore God to help us walk steadfastly and generously on the path of reconciliation and unity among all the disciples of Christ.

Preparation

A large candle/Easter candle may be placed in front, in the centre, and lit for the duration of the service.

ORDER OF SERVICE

Opening Hymn

Invitation to prayer*

Presider:	Lord, open our lips.
All:	**And we shall proclaim your praise.**

P:	Glory to God in the highest.
All:	**And peace to God's people on earth.**

(words of welcome)

Penitential Rite

---

* "Prayer in the Morning," in *Living with Christ*, Novalis, July 2003, p. 159.

P: The Lord Jesus taught us: "So when you are offering your gift at the altar, if you remember that your brother or sister has something against you,

All: **Leave your gift there before the altar and go: first be reconciled to your brother or sister, and then come and offer your gift."**

(moment of silence)

All: Repeat as above: **"Leave your gift . . ."**

P: May almighty God have mercy on us, forgive us our sins and bring us to everlasting life.

All: **Amen.**

Sharing the Peace

P: Peace of Christ!

All: Let us share each other's burdens.

(A greeting of peace is shared.)

Hymn of Praise

Psalm Praise

Psalm 33 (alternatively, Psalms 100 or 148; Psalm 51, on Fridays.)

Side 1: Rejoice in the Lord, O you righteous. Praise befits the upright.

S2: **Praise the Lord with the lyre; make melody to him with the harp of ten strings.**

S1: Sing to him a new song; play skillfully on the strings, with loud shouts.

S2: **For the word of the Lord is upright, and all his work is done in faithfulness.**

S1: He loves righteousness and justice; the earth is full of the steadfast love of the Lord.

S2: **By the word of the Lord the heavens were made, and all their host by the breath of his mouth.**

S1: He gathered the waters of the sea as in a bottle; He put the deeps in storehouses.

S2: **Let all the earth fear the Lord; let all the inhabitants of the world stand in awe of him.**

S1: For he spoke, and it came to be; He commanded, and it stood firm.

S2: **The Lord brings the counsel of the nations to nothing; he frustrates the plans of the peoples.**

S1: The counsel of the Lord stands for ever, the thoughts of his heart to all generations.

S2: **Happy is the nation whose God is the Lord, the people whom he has chosen as his heritage.**

S1: The Lord looks down from heaven; He sees all humankind.

S2: **From where he sits enthroned he watches all the inhabitants of the earth —**

S1: He who fashions the hearts of them all, and observes all their deeds.

S2: **A king is not saved by his great army; a warrior is not delivered by his great strength.**

S1: The war horse is a vain hope for victory, and by its great might it cannot save.

S2: **Truly the eye of the Lord is on those who fear him, on those whose hope is his steadfast love,**

S1: to deliver their soul from death, and to keep them alive in famine.

S2: **Our soul waits for the Lord; he is our help and shield.**

S1: Our heart is glad in him, because we trust in his holy name.

All: **Let your steadfast love, O Lord, be upon us, even as we hope in you.**

Psalm prayer*

P: Nourish your people, Lord,
for we hunger for your word.
Rescue us from the death of sin
and fill us with your mercy,
that we may share your presence
and the joys of all the saints.

All: **Amen.**

---

* *Liturgy of the Hours* III, according to the Roman Rite, Catholic Book Publishing Co., New York 1975, Psalm-prayer, p. 732.

LITURGY OF THE WORD

Acclamation of the Word
(stand, acclamation may be chanted)

P: Rejoicing in the real yet imperfect communion which joins us together,

All: **let us pay attention to the Good News!**

P: Journeying together toward full visible communion,

All: **let us harken to God's word!**

Reading
Ephesians 3:14-21 (or another reading)
"that you may be strengthened in your inner being"
(moment of silence)

Intercessions

(Presider introduces the prayer intentions.)

R: Giving thanks to almighty God for the real yet imperfect communion which binds us together, we pray to the Lord:

All: **Lord, hear our prayer.**

R: Thankful for the churches' faithfulness in discipleship, witness and gospel service, we pray to the Lord:

All: **Lord, hear our prayer.**

R: Begging God for the conversion and continual reformation of the churches, in docility to the Holy Spirit, we pray to the Lord:

All: **Lord, hear our prayer.**

R: Asking for the grace to re-commit ourselves to seek, with patience and humility, the visible unity of the Church as Christ wills it and by the means that he wills, we pray to the Lord:

All: **Lord, hear our prayer.**

R: That the churches may learn how to help carry each other's burdens, and give common service to the world that God loves and saves in Jesus Christ, we pray to the Lord:

All: **Lord, hear our prayer.**

(The presider concludes the intercessions.)

Our Father . . .

Closing prayer[*]

P: Lord, we praise you with our lips,
and with our lives and hearts.
Our very existence is a gift from you;
to you we offer all that we have and are.
We ask this through our Lord Jesus Christ,
your Son, who lives and reigns with you
and the Holy Spirit, one God, for ever and ever.

All: **Amen.**

---

[*] *Liturgy of the Hours* III, p. 967.

Sending Forth

P: As we go forth, let us remember to return to common prayer often. In common prayer our fellowship is nurtured, across denominational lines. In common prayer we are strengthened for common witness and service.

All: **Glory to God, whose power, working in us, can do infinitely more than we can ask or imagine. Glory to God from generation to generation, in the church, and in Christ Jesus, forever and ever. Amen** (cf. Eph. 3: 20-21).

Recessional
(hymn, or instrumental only)

11. Evening Prayer Together

Trusting adoration.
The community of disciples, returning all things to God,
in Christ, at the end of the day.

Orientation

Praying together in sincerity of heart brings the disciples of Christ into closer communion. It is the Holy Spirit who helps us to pray worthily, and indeed comes to pray within us when invited (cf. Rom. 8: 26-27).

At the end of the day — with its armful of grace, joys and sorrows, sin perhaps — it is "right and just" to come to prayer, acknowledging that we are "worthless slaves" (Lk 17: 10), yet, more deeply, adopted children of God (1 Jn. 3: 2). In union with Christ we offer and entrust our lives again to God, before we slip and faint into sleep.

Our common evening prayer also becomes a faithful act of seeking and yielding to the grace of mutual forgiveness, reconciliation and healing among imperfectly joined Christians.

Preparation

Gather in silence around the lit Easter candle. The presider or pastor takes his/her place.

ORDER OF SERVICE

Songs
(one or more congregational hymns)

Welcome and Call to Prayer

Penitential Rite

*(Presider invites spontaneous expressions of sorrow, confession, .
. . repentance . . . regarding church fellowship . . . our divisions . .
. etc. It is good to allow for a slow pace, moments of silence . . .)*

Presider: May almighty God have mercy on us, forgive us our
sins, and bring us to everlasting life.

All: **Amen.**

Sharing the peace

Presider: The peace of the Lord be with you always.

All: **And with your spirit.**

Presider: Let us offer each other the sign of peace.

(the peace is shared in the assembly)

Prayer *(as follows, or spontaneous)*

Presider: Lord God, we come to you in prayer as "day is done
and darkness falls from the wings of Night" (H.W.
Longfellow). In your ever faithful providence, watch
over your Church this night, and patiently continue
to bless all godly religions, all humanity, our blue
planet and the whole created universe. Help us to
be your faithful people, reconciled and seeking full
communion. We ask this in Jesus' name.

All: **Amen.**

Night Psalm: Psalm 91
"God, protector of the righteous"

Side 1:   You who live in the shelter of the Most High, who abide in the shadow of the Almighty,

Side 2:   **will say to the Lord, "My refuge and my fortress; my God in whom I trust."**

S1:   For he will deliver you from the snare of the fowler and from the deadly pestilence;

S2:   **he will cover you with his pinions, and under his wings you will find refuge;**

S1:   his faithfulness is a shield and a buckler.

S2:   **You will not fear the terror of the night, or the arrow that flies by day,**

S1:   or the pestilence that stalks in darkness, or the destruction that wastes at noonday.

S2:   **A thousand may fall at your side, ten thousand at your right hand, but it will not come near you.**

S1:   You will only look with your eyes and see the punishment of the wicked.

S2:   **Because you have made the Lord your refuge, the Most High your dwelling place,**

S1:   no evil shall befall you, no scourge come near your tent.

S2:   **For he will command his angels concerning you to guard you in all your ways.**

S1: On their hands they will bear you up, so that you will not dash your foot against a stone.

S2: **You will tread on the lion and the adder; the young lion and the serpent you will trample under foot.**

S1: Those who love me, I will deliver; I will protect those who know my name.

S2: **When they call me, I will answer them; I will be with them in trouble, I will rescue them and honour them.**

S1: With long life I will satisfy them, and show them my salvation.

(*pause*)

Scripture Reading (*proclaimed by one or two readers*)

Luke 24:13-35 (two voices)
or
Ephesians 1:17-20 or 3:14-19

Song (*a Taizé refrain, repeated*)

Short Reflection/Meditation or Witness
(*some silence*)

Intercessions (*spontaneous*)

The Lord's Prayer

Sending Forth

Presider: As we go forth, let us remember to return to common prayer often. In common prayer our fellowship is nurtured across denominational lines, and we are strengthened for common witness and service.

All: **Glory to God, whose power, working in us, can do infinitely more than we can ask or imagine. Glory to God from generation to generation, in the Church, and in Christ Jesus, forever and ever. Amen** (cf. Eph. 3: 20-21).

Recessional (*hymn, or instrumental only*)

DOXOLOGY

O God, mighty and immortal, we worship you in your holiness.
We praise you for your plan of mercy and immortal life for the
world, in and through Jesus Christ our Lord. We thank you for
the mystery which is your Church, born from the wounded side
of Christ on the cross and the outpouring of the Spirit over the
Church and the world. We thank you for your faithfulness in
calling us into the fellowship of your Son, Jesus Christ our Lord (cf.
1 Cor. 1: 9).

We ask your forgiveness for our many acts of unfaithfulness
along the centuries, for the wounds our divisions have inflicted
and continue to inflict on the Body of Christ. Help the churches
to grow in trusting obedience to the will and prayer of Christ for
unity, for the sake of the world you love. Lead and strengthen us on
the steady path of ecclesial conversion. May the Church resist the
temptation of self-centeredness. May she taste and share more fully
the joy of the Gospel!

We ask you to bless and protect the whole world, indeed all
worlds yet unknown, and to regenerate them in your grace. For we
know that "creation waits with eager longing . . . and will obtain the
freedom of the glory of the children of God" (Rom. 8: 19.21)

We, also, wait for the return in glory of your Christ, soon or in
thousands of years, and the fulfillment of your kingdom of saving
grace. Please keep hope alive and vibrant in the human heart as, in
accordance with your promise, we wait for a new heaven and a new
earth, where righteousness is at home (cf. 2 Pet. 3: 13).

To you, O God, be the glory of infinite Love, infinite Grace!
AMEN.

*(when praying alone, you are invited to make this prayer more
personal by praying it in the first person singular)*